To: Chicago
Sri. Dr. Marie A Scase

Blessings Abound!

Dec. 2.11

Rev. Dr. Seaman creatively uses the metaphor of the womb to help us understand the value and sacredness of destiny, vision, and purpose. Our womb has a treasure, a gift if you will, within it. It is the cradle of potential that births possibilities. There is greatness in the womb. Every woman has a womb story that tells all that God has spoken into her life. What God has spoken will come to pass. The womb is sacred and sanctified unto God and must be prepared to bring forth the promise of God. Rev. Seaman also issues a warning to each of us. She warns us not to allow others to abort what is in our womb. Don't abort the vision. Don't abort the purpose. Don't abort destiny. Don't allow that which is in your spiritual (and physical) womb to be aborted. The enemy wants to destroy the sacred contents of the womb because of the tremendous potential. Our wombs are pregnant with potential. This book encourages women to live life to the fullest, to realize our purpose, vision and destiny. Even through our tears God is birthing something. God is preparing each of us for the delivery. So my sisters, get ready! Your destiny is about to come forth!

The questions at the end of each chapter challenge the reader to examine and reexamine their thinking and understanding. The questions provide opportunities for journaling as well as individual and group Bible study.

Thanks again. Yes, my sister, I am continuing to walk in destiny, vision, purpose, and joy because I finally understand that I am favored of the Lord. Thank you Rev. Dr. Seaman for reminding us of God's plan and purpose for us. This book has blessed my life, and I plan to use it to bless the lives of other women.

—Rev. Dr. Yoreel Trumpet
Minister to Women
St. Luke AME Church
New York, NY

Luke 1:39–41 reveals to us that when Mary—who was pregnant and carrying the Messiah Jesus Christ—came in the presence of Elizabeth—who was carrying the forerunner, John the Baptist—the child in Elizabeth's womb was quickened in such a way that he jumped. These two women, who contained within them the promised children who would eventually be used to transform the world, had what can be defined as a *womb connection*: a connection so powerful that the child leaped, thereby attesting to the life-giving glory that their wombs possessed.

I believe that Dr. Maria Seaman has produced a powerful book that will give every reader a womb-quickening connection. As God uses this book, its powerful words will leap off the pages and touch the wombs of readers who will all be reminded of the power of vision, the steadfastness of God's promise, and the overflowing potential that is within them. Even readers whose dreams have long appeared to be dormant will be quickened and brought into the exciting and glorious hope that life will come forth from them.

Here, Dr. Seaman uses her life experiences as a wife, a mother, an educator, and a powerful evangelist to communicate her special and unique insights into the complex and profound issues of the womb, and what it takes to see the promises of God burst forth from potential into reality. I am confident that the individual lives of those who read this book will be touched, moved, stirred, and transformed as God uses this great work to bless them in profound ways.

As God uses this book to transform your life, may God bless you and everything that shall burst forth out of your womb.

—Reverend William A. Lee Jr.
Pastor, Heritage Worship Centre
New Testament Church of God
Hamilton, Bermuda

This book will challenge you, stretch you, and push you into understanding that just as the natural cycle of conception and birthing come with pain and agony...so does the spiritual cycle of conceiving and birthing the things that God has designed for our destiny.

If you are ready to grow up and become all that God declares you are, as well as do all that God purposes you to do...then this dynamic book by Rev. Dr. Maria Antoinette Seaman is for you. Her anointing as preacher/teacher along with her training in the science of biology comes across clear in this book. Read it...you won't be the same!

—Rev. Dr. Wanda A. Turner
Minister, Author, and Musician

From a background of both academic and spiritual excellence, Maria brings before us a snapshot of the life cycle of the natural womb, and the glorious knowledge of birthing the contents of our spiritual womb.

As you read the insightful and interesting presentation of these pages, you will be informed, challenged encouraged, and inspired to follow the biblical examples given in *The World of the Womb in God's Plan for Man*. I am sure readers will be blessed for the time they spend in these pages.

—Bishop Goodwin C. Smith, DD, DLitt, MBE, JP
Administrative Bishop, Bermuda

This book is more than a theological exegesis on the concept and consequences of a womb; it is a welcomed tool for biblical study and spiritual enrichment.

The soundness of its metaphorical intrigue will spur a revolution in thought and appreciation of the womb for generations to come.

I therefore endorse this timely work and recommend it highly. Well done, daughter in Zion!

—Bishop Vernon G. Lambe Sr., MBE, JP, DD
Senior Pastor, The Chapel of the Anointing
General Overseer, First Churches of God,
Bermuda

The discovery of unique spiritual concepts is a refreshing experience that stimulates the soul into action and revelation. Dr. Maria Seaman's book is an outstanding revelation that is certain to find a lodging place in the spirit of all who are spiritually pregnant, and who anticipate the birthing of holy purpose right where they live.

Wherever you are in your personal life is where you ought to be. It is from there that the holy process of God will begin to energize and propel you into the holy destiny that He planned for you, long before you were birthed from your mother's womb.

Dr. Seaman's book is filled with helpful wonderful explanations and teaching through revelation. She uncovers veiled truths that highlight the essentiality of recognizing our potential in God, and the divine plan and purpose that will take us into holy destiny and fulfillment through the "world of the womb."

Dr. Seaman's book will help you to experience the value that God has placed in your life for others, and ultimately for His glory. I believe that you will receive holy impartation by the Spirit of God as you read this life-changing book.

—Bishop M. Neville A. Smith, MBE, JP, FCMI
Bishop, International Fellowship
of Christian Churches
Pastor, Radnor Road Christian Fellowship
Bermuda

This book provides a rare look at the magnificent creative genius of the Creator and the perfect principles inherent in His creation. This work is a must for all who want to see life through the eyes of the Master of the womb—the Lord and Creator of all life.

—Dr. Myles E. Munroe
Bahamas Faith Ministries International
Nassau, Bahamas

The World of the Womb

in God's Plan for Man

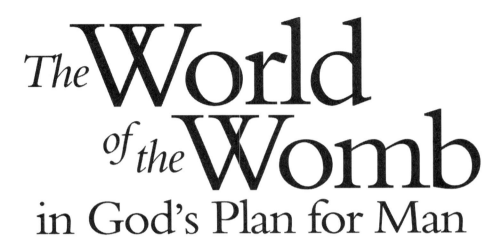

DR. MARIA ANTOINETTE SEAMAN

CREATION HOUSE
A STRANG COMPANY

THE WORLD OF THE WOMB IN GOD'S PLAN FOR MAN
by Dr. Maria Antoinette Seaman
Published by Creation House
A Strang Company
600 Rinehart Road
Lake Mary, Florida 32746
www.creationhouse.com

Unless otherwise noted, Scripture quotations are from the King James Version of the Bible.

Scripture quotations marked niv are from the Holy Bible, New International Version. Copyright © 1973, 1978, 1984, International Bible Society. Used by permission.

Cell drawing on page 19 from *God's Prescription for Healing* by James P. Gills, M.D., Lake Mary, FL: Siloam, 2004.

Cover design by Terry Clifton

Library of Congress Control Number: 2004117407
International Standard Book Number: 1-59185-792-9

05 06 07 08 09 — 987654321
Printed in the United States of America

I dedicate this book to my husband, Kent "Peter" Eugene Seaman, the three girls who have issued out of my womb (K'Maria, Jenna-Maria, and D'Hstiny), and to my three souls in heaven's womb. I also dedicate this book to my parents, Raymond and Dianne Russell Sr.

Contents

Foreword

IN THIS INSIGHTFUL book, Dr. Maria Seaman delivers a strikingly creative message regarding the "womb potential" of every individual. Within these pages is a treasure of wisdom awaiting those who wish to gain a better understanding of the awesome potential in all of us and Satan's desire to destroy that potential.

Humankind is made in the image of God. Therefore, there is within us a genetic connection, an automatic response, and an intuitive desire to do the will of God. It does not matter whether we acknowledge this, or live an ungodly life. There is yet within the "womb" of every individual a desire to connect and reconnect with God our Creator. The enemy works contrary to this plan. Satan's agenda has been, and will always be, to destroy the image and plan of God for our lives.

This book is straightforward in its content and style. The message is significantly insightful and profoundly practical. Armed with the truth of God's enduring Word, Seaman reminds us that every living person has a spiritual womb. The gift of creativity and the desire to "bring forth" has been housed in our minds, because we are like God, our Creator. We serve a God of creativity and each of us is accountable to God for the creativity He has placed within us. The implication is clear. We must bring forth the plan, purpose, and vision God has for our lives so that He might say, "Well done, thou good and faithful servant..." (Matthew 25:21).

Dr. Maria Seaman is a tremendous minister of the Gospel of Jesus Christ. I have observed the hand of God upon her life and ministry. She is a woman with a vision and passion to teach people the life-changing truths of the Word of God. To this end, she has devoted herself to helping others discover and reach their full potential in Christ. Dr. Seaman is an anointed and dedicated servant of the Lord, a loving wife, and a mother of three daughters. Her candor and commitment to excellence in ministry are noteworthy.

The World of the Womb in God's Plan for Man is Seaman's first book, and I am honored to provide the foreword. I regard her as a gifted sister in Christ and faithful minister of the gospel. With genuine excitement I commend this work to you!

—BISHOP MILLICENT H. HUNTER
THE BAPTIST WORSHIP CENTER CHURCH
PHILADELPHIA, PENNSYLVANIA

Introduction

A S A MEANS of carrying out His plan and His purpose for
individuals and for mankind, God has created the safe
and nourishing environments of two types of wombs, the
physical and the spiritual. Most people are familiar with the
wonder of the womb, or uterus, that is a part of the physical makeup of a woman's body. However, there are also other
wombs—the spiritual wombs, the places where hopes and
dreams are formed before they are brought forth.

Many of the same principles of the physical womb of a
woman apply to spiritual wombs. For example, just as there
is a great struggle between God and Satan over the physical
life a pregnant woman carries within her "natural" womb,

there is also a great struggle over the God-given hopes and dreams that a spiritually pregnant person carries within his/ her "spiritual" womb. Because mankind was created in the image of God, Satan works to destroy those images of Him. Also, in an effort to destroy the plans of God and replace them with his own, Satan works to thwart the growth and the birth of the dreams and the gifts that God has placed within individuals.

While these satanic attacks are taking place in bedrooms, boardrooms, courtrooms, and even within the rooms of the Christian church, God works through human vessels who will bring forth what is necessary for the fulfillment of His glorious plan for individuals and for mankind.

To be willing vessels through which God can bring forth this kind of life through our physical wombs or our spiritual ones, we must be willing to conceive, nurture, protect, and then labor to bring forth this life. We must also recognize, avoid, and even fight off threats to our womb and to what we are carrying.

Even if it seems like your own womb has been barren for a long time, you may rest assured that nothing in God goes wasted. If you are a willing vessel in which the presence of God dwells, He will surely bring life through you. The beauty of His timing is often seen in how He will bring spectacular life out of what once seemed barren, creating a testimony to the world that He can indeed do the seemingly impossible.

Today is a day for you to begin to celebrate what will be coming forth through you soon. By God's design, you are to play an important and integral part in the fulfillment of God's plan.

My hope in writing this book is that you will accept, recognize, cherish, nurture, protect, and bring forth all of the splendorous life that God has placed within you.

Chapter One

The Conclusion of the Matter

Remember the former things of old: for I am God, and there is none else; I am God, and there is none like me, declaring the end from the beginning, and from ancient times the things that are not yet done, saying, My counsel shall stand, and I will do all my pleasure.

—ISAIAH 46:9–10

WHY DO DRUNKARDS sitting on barstools sing gospel songs? Why do the most blatant sinners call on God when they are desperate for help? Why do women living lifestyles of sin thank God for their newborns? When suddenly confronted with a life crisis, why do haters of Christians ask Christians to pray for them? Why do drug addicts cry out to God for help every night just before they collapse into a stupor? Why are we blessed by hymns sung by people still clinging to sin?

These questions have been pondered by many even though they all have the same answer: every person has an inherent desire to please God. Regardless of whether a person is

3

conscious of it or not, he or she desires to connect with the *Elohim*—the Creator of the Universe. This connection that is housed within the spiritual womb of every man, woman, and child is similar to the connection of the unborn child to its mother. It is an umbilical connection that supplies the very life-substance by which each of us survives. Just as the unborn baby cannot help but receive from its mother, people—even those who are not serving God—cannot help but receive from their Father who created them in His own image.

> So God created man in his own image, in the image of God created he him; male and female created he them.
>
> —Genesis 1:27

Because each of us was made in the image of God, our inherent connection to Him perpetuates our intrinsic desire to please Him by being like Him. This natural connection and corresponding desire is what drives us to yield to God's will when the Holy Spirit initially draws us to redemption in Christ. When we who were dead in our sins bow our wills to the will of the Father in this way, our natural connection to our Father is unblocked and we receive abundant new life. When we have been made new in Christ and the spiritual umbilical cord is unblocked, life-sustaining nourishment from our Father flows to us and then through us.

The Bible clearly states that the only way a lost sinner can come to know the Father through the Son is by being drawn (or attracted) to the Son by the Holy Spirit. The same Spirit that moved over total darkness and emptiness before Creation is the same Spirit that now moves over dark and empty lives, drawing them to the foot of the Cross where their sin— their blockage from their eternal Father—will be forever removed by faith in the sin-cleansing power of the perfect sacrifice for sin, the perfect Lamb of God, Jesus Christ, the only begotten Son of God. This newness of life and unblocking of their umbilical cord to their Father restore them to their original purpose of pleasing God by being like Him and walking in His ways as they are led by His Spirit.

> For as many as are led by the Spirit of God, they are the sons of God.
> —ROMANS 8:14

> And such were some of you: but ye are washed, but ye are sanctified, but ye are justified in the name of the Lord Jesus, and by the Spirit of our God.
> —1 CORINTHIANS 6:11

> For by one Spirit are we all baptized into one body, whether we be Jews or Gentiles, whether we be bond or free; and have been all made to drink into one Spirit.
> —1 CORINTHIANS 12:13

Whether we like it or not, we are at the center of the struggle between Satan and God. It is the ultimate power struggle and because we resemble God and came out of His mind (or womb), we are Satan's targets. To feed his revenge over being cast out of heaven and to express his hatred of God, Satan plots ways to destroy those who were born in God's own image and have wombs from which to bring forth life that flows from Him. Christians must aim to stop the tide of the increase of hell, and thus it becomes important for all to undertand that we must do all within our power to bring about an understanding of the vitality of every womb on the earth.

THE ROAD MAP OF YOUR LIFE

Most books begin with the beginning, deliver the bulk of the story in the middle, and then end with the conclusion. However, God's order is different from this because He knows our ending when we are only beginning. To understand this comparison, read the following paragraph from beginning to end:

> Aoccdrnig to rscheearch at a uinervtisy, it deosn't mttaer In waht oredr the ltteers in a wrod are wirettn dwon. The olny iprmoetnt tihng that maettrs is taht the frist and lsat ltteer is at the rghit pclae. The rset can be a ttaol mses and you can siltl raed it wouthit a porbelm. Tihs is bcuseae we do not raed ervey lteter by itslef, but the mnid wlil raed the wrod as a wlohe. Tihs is amaznig! Do you blieeve it? I thnik you do!

Did you notice that even though many of the words were misspelled, you were able to read the paragraph without skipping a beat? As long as the first letter and the last letter of each word were in the correct places, reading the paragraph was easy even though the order of the letters in between the first and last letters of the word was incorrect. In other words, although the in-between was out of order or "messed up," the reading and comprehension of the content was possible because the beginning was right and the ending was right. Reading these misspelled words was possible because our minds read the word as a whole.

This example illustrates how God is able to read our lives. That is, in a way that is similar to how you compensated for the incorrect letters in the middle of each word by focusing on the correct letters at the beginning and end of each word. Because God knows the beginning and ending of the story of our lives, He can redeem our "in-betweens" so that the original meaning and purpose of our lives will be fulfilled and our testimony will bring Him glory.

Nothing catches God by surprise. What we are shocked by, God has already seen and dealt with because He knows what our end is. God is omniscient, which means He knows all things. Nothing escapes His mind or His will. In spite of our mess-ups and mistakes, He is the source of every component of life we need in order to walk out our inherent desire to please Him as vessels through which the essence of life in Him flows out to others.

Study Questions:

1. Have I allowed the "messed up" and "mixed-up" situations of my life to discourage me into believing that my dreams will never be realized?

2. Can God reinstate His divine plan for my life, in spite of the detours and dead ends that I have met up with?

3. What is my passion, my dream, or my vision?

4. Do I really believe that God has a plan for my life? If so, how can I go about uncovering and pursuing His plan?

Prayer

God, I thank You for leading me to read this book. Father, I pray that as I read each chapter, You will begin to show me a picture of what You have divinely placed within my own womb. Lord, I thank You because I have been created in Your image and have an abundance of creativity and potential within me. Now Father, guide me to birth that which is within me, so that my gift to the world may be witnessed and enjoyed by all. I ask this in the name of Your precious Son, Jesus Christ. Amen.

St. George's Hamilton

St. George's

Middle Road

South Shore

Hamilton

Somerset

Chapter Two

Life Choices—
Somerset

Here is a map of my home island of Bermuda. As you study this map, please note that:

1. There is only one island.

2. There are many streets, roads, and pathways.

3. Generally, there are several ways to get from one place to another.

There are options for getting from one place to another, both on the island of Bermuda and in life. For example, if we wanted to get from Somerset to St. George's, we could decide to take either South Shore Road or Middle Road.

Whether we are looking at a road map of an island or the map of life, if we haphazardly read either type of map or make unwise choices about the paths we choose, we may be delayed in our arrival or find hazardous conditions along the way that could otherwise have been avoided. The same is true of our choices in life. Our success or failure in life is dependent upon our making the right choices at the right places along our unique and personal map of life.

Because God is the Master Architect and Planner, your life could not possibly have been accidental. Even if your parents were surprised or shocked by the imminence of your birth, God was not. God already knew your beginning and your end before you were even born.

Since we know that God has mapped out our destination and best route, we quite naturally will want to know how to read this map so we can fulfill our inherent desire to please our Father.

> The steps of a good man are ordered by the LORD:
> and he delighteth in his way.
>
> —PSALM 37:23

Choosing the route we will take from God's roadmap is not nearly as simple as choosing a route on the map of an island. This is because we do not see the beginning, middle, or end of the journey all at once like God does. Therefore we must rely on Him to order our steps—one step at a time. Following His pathway, then, becomes the summation of moment-by-moment choices that will delight the Lord. This is only possible when His goodness shines through us and illuminates the way He would have us go. The light of Jesus shining through us also illuminates God's way to other people who may otherwise be in total darkness like the people were in darkness before the Savior was announced and revealed during Jesus' time here on earth.

It is very common to hear new Christians say that they wish they had made the decision to accept Jesus into their hearts long ago. This is because life without Jesus as Lord and Savior of one's life is no life at all. Instead, it is a fruitless life of stumbling around in darkness with no lantern showing the way. By His love and mercy, as the Lord directs us step-by-step on the pathway He has chosen for us to take to our destination, He will often use us as a vessel through which the Holy Spirit draws other people to Jesus Christ.

This lifestyle of obedience is not without struggle. Along with the struggles we face that are a product of the struggle between God and Satan over the souls (and the wombs) of man, we will also struggle against our own sinful (fleshly) desires. To overcome these struggles which would thwart us from fulfilling God's purposes for us, we must first be reconciled to the Father through His Son Jesus Christ and then thrive in our umbilical connection with God by getting to know Him.

Knowing God begins with being born again through Jesus Christ, who lived as an example of how we are to live life on earth and gave Himself up as on offering for our sins. To know God is to know His Word because the Word of God is a reflection of God Himself and Jesus Christ is the Word of God that was revealed in bodily form on earth. To walk in accordance with His direction, we must become familiar with God's nature and character, how He moves, and what He desires (and requires) us to do.

When Jesus was here on earth He did everything according to the will of His Father. Every time Jesus healed the sick, performed a miracle, or made someone whole it was according to His Father's will. This obedience to the Father is our example of how we are to live out our lives.

The ultimate showcase of Jesus' obedience to the will of His Father was when Jesus agonized over the crucial decision

He was to make in the Garden of Gethsemane. This is where Jesus pushed past his human emotions and fully embraced His divine womb that would bring forth spiritual life and liberty to the human race. When He embraced His divine womb, He made it possible for you and I to be born again.

> Saying, Father, if thou be willing, remove this cup from me: nevertheless not my will, but thine, be done.
> —LUKE 22:42

If we look even deeper into the life of Jesus, we see that He made a series of choices that all led up to the validity of that one ultimate choice. For example, His choice to be born of a woman and live a sinless life made it possible for the only perfect sacrifice for the sins of mankind to be made and the old covenant between God and man to be fulfilled. In that pivotal moment of the suffering and shame of the Cross being before Him, He made the ultimate decision to do the will of His Father in heaven rather than do what His human emotions and body were screaming at Him to do. So great was His pain over this decision that His sweat was as drops of blood.

The tug-of-war between the will of the Father and the will of our emotions and physical bodies (the flesh) is something we face to one degree or another each and every day. When this struggle challenges us, we can look to our perfect example Jesus Christ and be strengthened in the knowledge that He always made choices that were in accordance with the Father. We can also look to apostle Paul's biblical instructions for us to focus our attention and hearts on things of the Spirit rather than on the desires (or will) of the human flesh.

The Christian who chooses to remain dead to the desires of the flesh and instead live by the Spirit of God will walk very differently from those who choose otherwise. Like Jesus brought forth spiritual life through His many choices to obey the will of God rather than His human will, we will also be used by God to bring forth spiritual life if we consistently choose His will over the desires of the flesh.

> For they that are after the flesh do mind the things of the flesh; but they that are after the Spirit the things of the Spirit. For to be carnally minded is death; but to be spiritually minded is life and peace. Because the carnal mind is enmity against God: for it is not subject to the law of God, neither indeed can be. So then they that are in the flesh cannot please God.
> —ROMANS 8:5–8

Another struggle we all face is God's way versus the ways of our popular culture. In Joshua 24:15, we read Joshua's declaration that he has chosen God's path instead of the common or popular one. Here, he declares that he and his family will serve the Lord. We are presented with this same choice every day—God's way or the more popular way?

> And if it seem evil unto you to serve the LORD, choose you this day whom ye will serve; whether the gods which your fathers served that were on the other side of the flood, or the gods of the Amorites, in whose land ye dwell: but as for me and my house, we will serve the LORD.
> —JOSHUA 24:15

The honorable men of the Old and New Testaments are highly esteemed in Scripture because of the choices they made that were in accordance with the will of God. Reading about the lives of Abraham, Joseph, Daniel, David, Elijah, Ezekiel, John the Baptist, apostle Paul, and others provide us with examples of what God was able to do through yielded vessels whose choices consistently demonstrated God's character and His ways. While it is true that mistakes made by some of these men are also recorded in Scripture, it is also true that we can learn from how these same men made adjustments and were reestablished on the path God had appointed for them.

By getting to know God, discovering what pleases Him, being instructed by His Word, learning from the biblical examples of how He led the saints who went before us, modeling Jesus Christ, and yielding to the Holy Spirit, our steps will be ordered by Him as we fulfill our destiny in our journey toward our heavenly home.

STUDY/DISCUSSION QUESTIONS

1. Examine past decisions and discuss how these choices shaped and formed your present.

2. Are there any course corrections that you can and should make now or in the future?

3. How will you change the way and attitude with which you make choices?

4. In what areas of your life do you have the most tug-of-war between the will of God and the will of the flesh?

5. What changes in your life do you need to make to get to know God and His ways better?

Prayer

Lord, I thank You because You are such a forgiving Father. Today I come to You because I need You to forgive me for the many mistakes I have made. Lord God, there have been many times that through the power of my tongue I have disagreed with Your holy Word and have ordered my own steps. Lord, today I submit myself to Your plan and I ask You to make your way plain to me. Father, again I thank You for allowing me to start afresh. Keep me aware of the traps and pitfalls that the enemy has and will set before me. Give me the wisdom to obey the Spirit rather than my own flesh. Quicken me to identify and choose Your ways rather than the ways of the popular culture. I thank You for every way of escape. In Jesus' name, I pray. Amen.

Chapter Three

God Is Organized

And the earth was without form, and void; and darkness was upon the face of the deep. And the Spirit of God moved upon the face of the waters.

—Genesis 1:2

THE VERY ESSENCE of God is that He is a God of order. In the very beginning, God called the entire world into order. When God called forth order out of disorderliness, He called into existence in a physical state what He already is and ever shall be. This principle establishes the fact that we who were created in the image of God can only create, make, or form what is already within us.

Because there is no emptiness or void in God, whatever He speaks forth will be revealed. In other words, God's Word can never return to Him void. Since God's Word is a creative Word, what He says already is. Whether we believe God's Word does not and cannot cancel out the effect or the impact of the creative power of His life-filled Word.

This orderliness may be seen in the fact that when the Word became flesh, this Word (Jesus Christ) was actually a picture of the Father, so much so that Jesus said that in seeing Him the Father is seen. Consequently, what Jesus did on earth was in perfect order with His Father's will.

We can also see the orderliness of God as we look at the organization of the universe as it relates to human beings:

> Universe → Earth → Continents → Seas → Islands → Parishes → Communities → Neighborhoods → Homes → Families → Individuals

Usually, we stop at the individual when we diagram the order of the universe in this way. However, we can diagram even further to view how He has ordered the makeup of mankind:

Nucleus
Cytoplasm
Ribosomes
Mitochondria
Vacuole
Golgi Apparatus
Endoplasmic Reticulum
Lysosomes

> Individuals → Body Systems → Organs → Tissues → Cells

It can therefore be said that the smallest living part of the entire universe is the cell. Since man was made in the image of God it would follow that we should be able to see the reflection of God in this basic component of life, the cell.

As we examine the inner workings of the cell, keep in mind that God created (and organized) this smallest living thing.

THE CELL

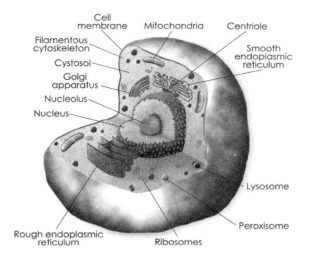

Cell membrane Mitochondria Centriole
Filamentous cytoskeleton
Cystosol
Golgi apparatus
Nucleolus
Nucleus
Smooth endoplasmic reticulum
Lysosome
Peroxisome
Rough endoplasmic reticulum Ribosomes

The cell is made up of the following components:

1. The nucleus: The ruler of the kingdom. The nucleus is in charge of all that goes on inside the cell. The nucleus is the "brain" or the control center of the cell's activity.

2. The mitochondria: The workers or the power-houses of the cell. The mitochondria will carry out the job that has been given to them and allow the cell to accomplish its internal activities.

3. The endoplasmic reticulum (ER): The passageways or the roadway system. The ER allows substances to move through them to get where they need to be.

4. The ribosomes: The builders of protein. The ribosome makes proteins that are needed for the structure and repairing of cell tissue.

5. The golgi apparatus: The factory building. This is where many substances are stored in packaging.

6. The cytoplasm: The water environment. The cytoplasm is the medium through which all of the activity takes place. Also, all of the structures within the cell reside within the cytoplasm.

7. The lysosomes: The garbage collectors. Because there is a great amount of activity within the cell, there are waste products that need to be cleaned up. This is the role of the lysosomes.

8. The cell membrane: The city walls. The cell membrane provides structure and is the door or point of entrance for substances to leave or enter the cell.

This description of these components and corresponding functions show that the cell is not a mindless entity. On the contrary, it is well organized in structure and in how it functions. In the cell, in this minute component of human life, we see the important characteristic of the Father that we have been focusing on in this chapter—organization. Even the smallest component of mankind is a reflection of the mind of God!

> For I know the thoughts that I think toward you, saith the LORD, thoughts of peace, and not of evil, to give you an expected end.
> —JEREMIAH 29:11

Every nucleus, every "brain" of every cell of a person's body, contains all of that person's genetic information. This blueprint of genetic information is called DNA. The person's makeup is determined by this blueprint. The blueprint of each person was designed by the Master Architect and Planner.

To understand how the blueprint of our makeup relates to

the choices we make on the road map of life, we will examine how the cell will malfunction if its organized environment is disturbed. For instance, if a person is in the desert and water is not available, this spells trouble because the human body is nearly 70 percent water and each of its cells is mostly water. If the water released through perspiration is not replaced, the cells will begin to malfunction. When the water within the cells is depleted, the nuclei of the cells cannot give out the right instructions. Therefore, this person (without water) in the desert will then begin to experience hallucinations. This means that the brain of the person begins to see what it desires, rather than what is. The delirious person whose cells are malfunctioning will see mirages of water that are not really there or oases where there are none. The person thinks the fulfillment of his/her needs is within reach when in fact it is just more scorching sand.

It could be said that when this happens, the cell is "out of its mind." The cell is out of control because it cannot function properly without the needed water. We can also take this illustration even further and see the importance of our umbilical cord to God. Without the water of the Word of God, our spiritual cells will begin to malfunction and we will begin to see things that are not really there. Oftentimes, we will become deluded by the notion that we are self-sufficient and have all that we need, when in reality we are drying up and losing our ability to function. To see things as they really are—to see things as God sees them—we must be continually replenished by and reliant upon the Living Word of God.

Study/Discussion Questions

1. Have your assessments of yourself and your potential taken into consideration the fact that you are created in the image of God?

2. How can knowing that God designed the blue-print contained in every cell of your body change how you see yourself and your potential?

3. Has your view of yourself and your potential been distorted because you have not been see-ing yourself as God sees you?

4. How can valuing yourself as being minutely designed by God affect the choices in life that you will make?

5. What steps can you take to see things God's way so that He can direct your steps in life that He has designated for you?

PRAYER

Father, thank You for designing me in a way that makes it fully possible for me to walk in Your ways and accomplish Your will. Thank You for creating me in Your image. Thank You for designing me to be a reflection of You. Where my vision has been clouded by delusions of self-sufficiency, please help me to see through Your eyes so that I may bring delight to You and finish the course that You have set before me. Lord, let me be a reflection of You and let my life be a means of showing others Your ways, for Your Word tells us that the steps of a good man are ordered by You. In Jesus' name, I pray. Amen.

Chapter Four

The Wonder–filled and Water–filled World of the Womb

For I know the thoughts that I think toward you, saith the LORD, thoughts of peace, and not of evil, to give you an expected end.

—JEREMIAH 29:11

THE JOURNEY OF THE WOMB

BECAUSE GOD HAS designed us to house, nourish, and bring forth that which is physical as well as that which is spiritual, it is important for us to understand the lifecycle of the womb. Understanding the physical womb, or uterus, will help us understand how spiritual wombs function.

The womb is prepared and equipped.

The womb has been uniquely designed for one purpose: to bring forth fruit. Its every muscle and every tissue are designed to bring forth new life. This new life will be the "image" of God Almighty.

The womb is nourished.

The womb is not a sedentary place. There is always activity in the womb. It is constantly nourished with a fresh supply of blood. It is this fresh supply of blood that fills the walls of the womb in order to give proper nutrition to the growing cells of a new life. Each month, if this fresh blood supply is not put to use (with a new pregnancy), then this blood is released out of the body and preparation is made for a new beginning. This new beginning or new cycle is known as the cycle of life or the menstrual cycle.

The womb is available and ready.

The womb sits in a matured female body. It is when this female has matured and has experienced secondary sexual characteristics that the womb is available to receive that one fertilized cell that will become a fetus and then a baby.

The womb is a place of security.

There is no other more protected place than the womb of a woman. For this place is a sacred place that houses the greatest potential of all. Who knows if this sacred place will bring forth a doctor, a minister, a mechanic, a teacher, a banker, or other major contributor to the lives of others. This place of security needs much care and protection, for there can be no under-standing or comprehension of the totality of what God will allow to come forth out of this place. The mind of man cannot fathom what God has already planned for this fertilized seed.

The womb is a place of growth potential.

Growth is an automatic function of the womb, this special place that has the potential of housing a baby. As the baby grows in this nourishing and protective place and as it is pre-pared to enter the world outside the womb, the womb grows and signals that new life is growing inside of it. As time moves on, the womb will tell a simple story. The essence of this story is that only God can truly understand the growth process occurring within the womb. Doctors still seek to understand and explain this growth, but they will never be able to fully explain its working mechanisms. Certainly, who but God—the Master Architect and Planner—can possibly understand how the growth of one fertilized seed leads to the appearance of a fully-developed human being?

The womb welcomes continual expansion.

Not only is there a physical expansion occurring within the womb itself, but there is also another type of expansion. This is the expansion of the minds of the mother and the people around her. For the woman whose womb is filled with unlimited potential begins to envision the possibilities! The people close to her wonder what will this new life become? This is the great hope that results from the possibilities of the womb.

The womb is destined for greatness.

The womb is a very interesting place. As we watch the exterior of the mother's body, we see evidence that the uterus is growing and we may even see the movement of the life growing within it. Before it empties itself of its precious cargo, the uterus is declaring that the new life will soon be living out his/her own story!

The womb contains hidden potential.

Even though we cannot see the baby or tell what the life story of this baby will be, we know that this baby has great potential. The baby within the uterus is growing according to the blueprint designed by the heavenly Father. The mother can protect the baby's housing and guard its nourishment, but by and large the mother must just "go with the flow" and trust that all will go as God planned. This principle also holds true after the child is born. The mother can protect the child's environment and work to ensure that the child's nourishment is healthful; however, by and large she will have to trust that the story of the child's life will unfold according to God's plan. Even the parents who follow God's instruction in Proverbs 22:6 to train up children in the way they should go will entrust God with the outcome of their children's lives.

The womb experiences a time for expulsion.

Isn't it interesting how whatever we may have is really not for us, but is for other people? This principle also begins in the womb. For although the expectant mother has housed this little one in her own body, at the God-appointed time she can no longer keep the baby to herself. This baby, filled with potential, must be released to bring joy to others. Consequently, there is a time for expulsion. What is within must come out! The baby, as comfortable as it has been inside the womb, cannot continue to grow and develop in this insulated place of incubation. Enough is enough. It is now time for expulsion and the baby needs even more room to develop. No mother ever desires to be pregnant forever, for at some point and time, even she becomes uncomfortable with the growth. Rather than being joyfully pregnant, the mother becomes increasingly uncomfortable. Even the woman who has been enjoying pregnancy comes to a point when she knows that the potential within must now be released.

The womb pain that precedes provision.

The final statement of any womb would have to be that its last chapter in housing a developing child is all about pain. This pain is an indicator that labor has begun, is continuing, and has ended. Pain is even present in the days after the womb has emptied its treasure. The birthing of anything that is within the womb involves pain: pain before, during, and after the new life is brought forth. Later, we will examine some of the ways in which this is also true when other types of new life are brought forth.

The womb experiences painful expansion.

During labor, areas of the body that may not have experienced growth in the past will now grow. As the potential of the womb is about to appear, areas that are about to receive this potential must enlarge themselves. In order for the baby to be born, the cervix and the mouth of the vagina must dilate.

The womb's powerful push!

Everything within the woman must now experience the push of a lifetime! It is with this final muscular contraction and push that the full potential of the womb is expelled. The womb cannot house this greatness forever. To be seen in its fullest potential, the child must be liberated to the bigger womb of the world.

The womb presents its present.

What a gift! What a present! The expectant father and mother have long awaited the presentation of their baby into their waiting arms. At last their dream of tenderly holding what had been within the womb has been fulfilled. This is the greatest present of the womb.

The conclusion to the story of the womb.

In delivering a healthy baby boy or baby girl, the womb has carried out its job to the fullest. Now it is time for the parents to continue the job of nurturing this life of potential until it can take care of itself.

The DNA of the child is made up of half of the father's DNA and half of the mother's DNA. This DNA combination results when the woman's ovaries release a mature egg during ovulation. This mature egg contains half of her deoxyribonucleic acid—DNA. This egg's blueprint for life is not complete because it only has half of the mother's genetic material. Therefore this egg needs a helpmate. It needs the rest of the information that will make it complete. Therefore during sexual intercourse (this word suggests that the sperm must follow an internal course or map), each spermatozoon of the sperm has a beginning location and it has a final destination. The goal of each spermatozoon is to reach the woman's egg, which is its other half because, like the egg only has half of the woman's genetic information, each spermatozoon only contains half of the man's genetic information.

It is interesting to note that even before the egg and the spermatozoon meet, there is an internal struggle to find the right way to go. Yes, even before the spermatozoon finds its way to the egg and penetrates it, there is a struggle as it seeks to fulfill its purpose and destiny. The struggle lies in the fact that not all of the spermatozoon will make it to the egg. Some get lost on the way. Some are deformed and do not get clear instructions from their nuclei. Some are simply not mobile enough to reach the destination. Most, however, are not fast enough to reach the destination before the egg is fertilized by another spermatozoon and the opportunity is closed forever.

Only one spermatozoon out of an average of nine million will reach the destination and penetrate the egg first. At the moment that this one sperm reaches and penetrates the membrane of the egg, a barrier is set up. Why is a barrier set up? Why a seal? Why this immediate protection? Because when one half meets its other half, their purpose, their fate, their destiny is sealed. The makeup of the fertilized egg is now permanent. This cell now contains all of its genetic makeup and its purpose is sealed for eternity. No other sperm can join this fertilized egg. There can be no mix-up or confusion in this matter. This is why DNA testing is so accurate. For once the sperm of a male joins with the egg of the female, no other male's sperm will be associated genetically with this zygote (fertilized egg).

STUDY/DISCUSSION QUESTIONS

1. Which people did God place in your life to nourish you in your earlier years?

2. Have you ever felt disadvantaged because of who your parents were/are? Discuss how you feel about the parents that God chose for you.

3. In what ways is each step essential to bringing about a natural birth?

4. How are the stages of giving birth to a spiritual baby—a dream, a vision, a hope, or the fruit of a ministry—similar to the stages of giving birth to a natural child?

5. Do you feel that you are pregnant with a spiritual baby like those described in the question above? If so, in what ways is what you are carrying in your spiritual womb being nourished?

6. Development of the zygote (egg fertilized by the sperm) takes nine months. These months are divided into trimesters (three months each). Each trimester is very unique from the other. Spiritually, which trimester are you in? How long have you been there? When do you see yourself moving to the next stage?

PRAYER

Dear Lord, once again I thank You for the miracle of life, both physical life and spiritual life. As I look over my life, I do not understand why You positioned me where You did. I put my trust in You and accept that You know what was and what is best. Only You know my beginning and my end all at the same time. I trust that Your purposes for me are good and You will birth through me all that is necessary for me to fulfill all of my purposes in You, Lord. I want to walk in Your perfect will and do the work that You have called me to do. In Jesus' name, I pray. Amen.

Chapter Five

God's Vision
and Conversation

Then the word of the LORD came unto me, saying, Before I formed thee in the belly I knew thee; and before thou camest forth out of the womb I sanctified thee, and I ordained thee a prophet unto the nations. Then said I, Ah, Lord GOD! behold, I cannot speak: for I am a child. But the LORD said unto me, Say not, I am a child: for thou shalt go to all that I shall send thee, and whatsoever I command thee thou shalt speak. Be not afraid of their faces: for I am with thee to deliver thee, saith the LORD. Then the LORD put forth his hand, and touched my mouth. And the LORD said unto me, Behold, I have put my words in thy mouth. See, I have this day set thee over the nations and over the kingdoms, to root out, and to pull down, and to destroy, and to throw down, to build, and to plant.

—JEREMIAH 1:4–10

IN THE PREVIOUS chapter we examined the fact that once the spermatozoon fertilizes the egg, the fate of the union is sealed. With this in mind, we begin to understand that God sees each and every man and woman as being complete. While we wait for life to unfold, God already has sealed the fate of every person. God did this when He chose which sperm would combine with which particular egg to form a unique human being. This means that while we wonder what an individual is capable of and what they will accomplish, God already knows what the end is. This can be seen as we take a look at different Bible passages and see how God spoke to the finished work rather than the present work. The Scriptures illustrate how God speaks to what He has made and completed, rather than to what remains to be lived out.

For instance, we can sum up a conversation that God has with Jeremiah when God says, "Boy, you see what you look like as you look into a mirror, but I see you as a completed work which I have made from the foundation of the world. Jeremiah, you say that you cannot speak, but I know what I have placed in you. What is in you are my words. Let me touch your mouth" (Jeremiah 1:4–6, author's paraphrase).

A little later we read that God touched Jeremiah's mouth and Jeremiah spoke! Why? First God spoke to what was already within Jeremiah. God stirred up the gift that had been dormant within Jeremiah. Jeremiah could not see what was inside of him or his potential, but God had formed Jeremiah and knew what He was speaking to and speaking about.

Then God touched Jeremiah's mouth, the place where the gift of speaking would be evident. (There is no way that God can touch a person and there not be a change! Not only will there be a change, but the change is sure to be evident to others.) Immediately after touching Jeremiah, God tested Jeremiah by giving him an opportunity to speak.

> Moreover the word of the LORD came unto me, say-
> ing, Jeremiah, what seest thou? And I said, I see a
> rod of an almond tree. Then said the LORD unto me,
> Thou hast well seen: for I will hasten my word to per-
> form it. And the word of the LORD came unto me the
> second time, saying, What seest thou? And I said, I
> see a seething pot; and the face thereof is toward the
> north.
>
> —JEREMIAH 1:11–13

God asked Jeremiah what he saw. Jeremiah was able to see and speak. When he told God what he saw, God encouraged him by applauding his response. God continued to "test" Jeremiah in this way and Jeremiah discovered that he had what it took to do what he thought he would not be able to do.

If we look through the eyes of faith in our perfect Provider, we will be looking through God's eyes so that we will be able to see that He has already prepared the way for us. Without faith, we will see ourselves through our own skewed and limited vision. We may look at ourselves and see a mess! However, God sees a message that must come forth. Jeremiah might have seen a mass of immaturity, but God looked beyond the youthfulness and saw Jeremiah's usefulness.

God will always test what is within us as a means of showing us what is there. Since each of our provisions for fulfilling our purpose was placed in us by Him, He knows exactly what to expect of us. Even if other people's expectations of us are low, God expects to see those gifts revealed and put to use. When our mother's egg met up with our father's spermatozoon, our destiny was fixed. From there, a lifetime of choices will determine whether that potential will be fully realized. Because God's expectations of us are high, He will deal with us as though He is expecting all He placed within us to come forth to full fruition.

Declaring the end from the beginning, and from ancient times the things that are not yet done, saying, My counsel shall stand, and I will do all my pleasure.
—ISAIAH 46:10

STUDY/DISCUSSION QUESTIONS

1. We often see ourselves as unworthy or incapable of attaining great heights. Think about your past. What occurrences have helped you to surmise that you cannot attain certain heights in the workplace, home, church, school, or community?

2. What unique gift(s) do you possess? (We may have the same talents, but no two people will manifest these talents in exactly the same way.)

3. Have you ever been "touched" by God? (That is, spiritually motivated or driven by God's Spirit to do a particular thing.) If so, how did you feel? And was this "touch" enough to energize you to complete the mission that God had laid on your heart?

4. Was there a time when you failed to accomplish something important to you? Did you feel that you failed God, or that God failed you?

5. Do you believe that you have everything you need within you to succeed in life? If so, are you walking in this success? If not, what can you do to nourish and bring forth what you need in order for you to succeed?

6. What situations has God used to test you and show you the maturity level of what He has placed within you?

7. Right now, do you see with the eye of faith what God has planned for your future? How can this vision help to bring about the manifestation of that plan?

PRAYER

Father, My God. I love You with my whole heart. Lord, I recognize that with every new day, You have given me a fresh new opportunity to see as You see. Lord, today I ask You to fix my sight, that I may see and then do those things which are pleasing to You. Lord, I admit that at times I have relied too much on my natural sight, and this has caused me to miss out on what You had planned for me. Father, I ask that You would be my guide and that the Holy Spirit would lead and guide me into all truth. Father, I thank You for giving me another chance to bring forth all that You have placed within me. Amen.

Chapter Six

Womb-Wonderful Stories

REBEKAH'S WOMB-WONDERFUL STORY

> And the LORD said unto her, Two nations are in thy womb, and two manner of people shall be separated from thy bowels; and the one people shall be stronger than the other people; and the elder shall serve the younger. And when her days to be delivered were fulfilled, behold, there were twins in her womb.
> —GENESIS 25:23–24

Rebekah had been barren. This state of barrenness was sad. There is nothing more devastating than a woman who desires to conceive and yet she cannot. In the verse preceding the passage above, Rebekah's husband takes responsibility and speaks to God on behalf of his barren wife. Following this, the Lord answers his prayer. (I must point out here that it is very commendable to see that the husband prayed and interceded on his wife's behalf. This shows headship and leadership in this family.) Evidently Isaac dearly loved the beautiful Rebekah and did not want her to have to bear this deep sorrow.

During the pregnancy Rebekah felt a lot of activity within her womb. When she asked the Lord about this, He told her that she was carrying twins. Rebekah was carrying fraternal twins. These twins were of the same mother and father, but their genetic makeups were very different. Their physical appearances as well as their temperaments would be very different.

The battling within her womb was a prophetic indicator of what was to come. What was occurring within the womb of Rebekah was a picture of what would occur once these boys entered the womb of the world. What happened when the baby boys were delivered pictured how they would live. Although Esau came out first and therefore was the elder of the two, Jacob came out right behind him and was holding onto Esau's heel. Later in life Jacob would also be right on Esau's heels, awaiting the opportunity to overtake him.

This overtaking did happen when Jacob bartered with Esau for his elder inheritance and then deceived his father into giving the inheritance to him instead of the elder brother Esau.

Perhaps since Rebekah had experienced such war within her womb, she should have prepared herself for what would be for her sons. Or perhaps Rebekah could have used the womb experience to learn that rather than create more division between her sons, she should seek to unite them in some way. Or perhaps Rebekah could have shared her concerns with her husband. In any case, this account shows us that even before the entrance into the world's womb, life in the mother's womb has its end set. God knows our beginning and end just like He already knew Jacob and Esau's beginning and end while they were still in the womb. God speaks to us and gives us prophetic pictures for a reason; therefore, we must be listening and watching for what He has to say. We can begin interceding in prayer over what He reveals to us. We can also begin searching for His guidance on how to prepare for and respond to what is to come.

RACHEL'S WOMB-WONDERFUL STORY

> And God remembered Rachel, and God hearkened to her, and opened her womb. And she conceived, and bare a son; and said, God hath taken away my reproach: And she called his name Joseph; and said, The LORD shall add to me another son.
> —GENESIS 30:22–24

Here we have it yet again. Rachel is another woman who had to bear the indignity of the inability to bring forth seed. Though Rachel had been Jacob's first choice, she was not first in being married to him or first in the ability to bring forth his seed. Rachel's older and far less attractive sister Leah had the honor and privilege of marrying Jacob first and of bearing his children first.

Yet, in addition to loving Rachel more than Leah, Jacob also loved the seed from Rachel's womb more than he loved the children from Leah. This would set in motion events that would affect whole nations. Like Rebekah, another prophecy was at work when Rachel's faith was broadened as God opened her womb to bring forth her firstborn. She named him "Joseph" which means "to add." By naming her firstborn "to add," Rachel was declaring that God would give her added children.

This was a picture of what God was going to do for His people. For through Joseph (once he had moved from the pit and into the palace), God would "add" to Jacob's house and take away the reproach of famine from the nation of Israel. So one more time, the womb tells a prophetic story that later unfolds in the lifetime of the offspring.

MANOAH'S WIFE'S WOMB-WONDERFUL STORY

> And the angel of the LORD appeared unto the woman, and said unto her, Behold now, thou art barren, and bearest not: but thou shalt conceive, and bear a son. Now therefore beware, I pray thee, and drink not wine nor strong drink, and eat not any unclean thing: For, lo, thou shalt conceive, and bear a son; and no razor shall come on his head: for the child shall be a Nazarite unto God from the womb: and he shall begin to deliver Israel out of the hand of the Philistines.
> —JUDGES 13:3–5

Here we have another barren woman. This barrenness is not to be seen and understood solely to be a temporary state or condition, but as it really was. In the eyes of men, it was an irreversible condition, a shameful state from which there was no escape.

However, God was not (and is not) limited by the viewpoint of mere men. When the Lord speaks into any hopeless, barren, empty situation or place, it will begin to bring forth life. For in the voice of God is creativity. If God speaks a Word, it already is so. This is why faith is so very important. For when we know that God has spoken something to us, even something that seems implausible, we must hold on to the word tightly in faith, through struggles with Satan, and struggles with our own flesh until the fulfillment of that word can be seen.

In the case of the wife of Manoah, a messenger comes and speaks on behalf of the Lord. This messenger is trustworthy because this angel has just left the presence of God to carry this prophetic word. The angel speaks not only into the life of this couple, but also into the life of this not yet conceived child. Do you get it? The couple has not even "gotten pregnant" when this divine messenger spoke to a work that was not completed. Why? Because God sees things in their completed state.

The angel gives a threefold message: 1. The Message of the Present Truth—this states that Manoah's wife is barren; 2. The Message of the Truth to Come—Manoah's wife shall conceive and bare a son; and 3. The Message of the Needed Truth—this son must be sanctified in a particular manner because he has been chosen to begin to deliver the nation of Israel from the bondage of the Philistines.

This child had a sacred and vital mission that required certain stipulations. This male child, Samson, was to not drink wine nor strong drink, not eat any unclean thing, and not have a razor touch his head.

Now it must be noted here that the stipulations began with Samson's mother. She was not to drink wine or strong drink, to not eat of any unclean thing, and to not allow any razor to touch Samson's head. The sanctifying process or the way by which Samson was to be set apart began while he was in the uterus or womb. Actually, the instructions were given before the conception took place. For if Samson's mother had taken of any wine or strong drink or had eaten any unclean thing, these things would have passed from her to her unborn child through the umbilical cord.

It is also interesting to note that even after Samson was born and was maturing, the stipulation was still in effect for the mother. That is, even as Samson grew up, his mother was still to abide by the instructions given to her by the messenger. In Samuel 14:9 we read of a tragic moment when Samson gives his father and his mother honey to eat. This honey has been taken out of the carcass of a dead lion, and is therefore unclean. So unbeknownst to Samson's parents, they have just broken their vow.

This mother, who had cherished her womb and protected her unborn son, could in no way stop his demise. For Samson's desire for unclean women led to his meal of unclean honey and later his actions would lead to the removal (by razor) of his hair.

Before he was even conceived, Samson's future was bright. However, once out of the protected environment of the womb, Samson became vulnerable to the outside world. This mother no longer had the ability to keep Samson from his own demise. Although this womb story is marred with tragedy, it did end with some degree of glory because Samson killed more Philistines during the final moments before his death than he had during all the other years of his life.

NAOMI'S WOMB-WONDERFUL STORY

> And Naomi said, Turn again, my daughters: why will ye go with me? are there yet any more sons in my womb, that they may be your husbands?
> —RUTH 1:11

Here we have the timeless story of Ruth and Naomi. At the beginning of this account, Naomi can be seen as being very fruitful because she had a husband, Elimelech; and two sons, Mahlon and Chilion. This began to change, however, when the entire family moved to Moab and her husband Elimelech died. The sons married women of that land and they continued to dwell there for ten years, but then her sons also died. All that Naomi had brought forth was gone. While there is now no fruitfulness of Naomi's natural womb, we will see that there was still fruitfulness in her spiritual womb.

With no hope of any more fruit coming from her own womb, Naomi determines to send her daughters-in-law back to their homelands as a way of giving them the opportunity to remarry and have children of their own. Both daughters-in-law weep at the thought of departing from Naomi, but only Ruth ultimately refuses to depart from Naomi. When Ruth and Naomi return to Judah, circumstances seem grim for them. When Naomi had set out from her homeland, she had been young, beautiful, married, and a mother. Now, with no male seed to her name, she faces a life of poverty. Upon her return, she asks the people to no longer call her "Naomi." Instead, she wants them to call her "Marah," which means "bitter."

This is where we see God do something with the womb of Naomi's heart. God allows Naomi to instruct her daughter-in-law on how to behave in the presence of others. As a result, Ruth married Boaz and from the fruit of that union, the womb of Naomi's heart is satisfied. In fact, Scripture tells us that when Obed was born to Ruth and Boaz, the women of the town said that Naomi had born a son:

> And the women her neighbours gave it a name, saying, There is a son born to Naomi; and they called his name Obed: he is the father of Jesse, the father of David.
>
> —RUTH 4:17

This child out of the womb (desire) of Naomi was the forefather of our Lord and Savior, Jesus Christ. For Obed begot Jesse, and Jesse begot David, and from that bloodline came Jesus the Christ. In this record, we see the compassion of God exhibited in how He worked (and works) on behalf of a dry womb. We also see another testimony of the fact that with God, nothing is impossible.

In summation, if it seems that what you desire is not possible, remember Naomi and Ruth. Perhaps God wants to use your Ruth to bring forth the blessing of your heart, which will bless you and generations to come.

Hannah's Womb-Wonderful Story

> And when the time was that Elkanah offered, he gave to Peninnah his wife, and to all her sons and her daughters, portions: But unto Hannah he gave a worthy portion; for he loved Hannah: but the Lord had shut up her womb. And her adversary also provoked her sore, for to make her fret, because the Lord had shut up her womb. And as he did so year by year, when she went up to the house of the Lord, so she provoked her; therefore she wept, and did not eat. Then said Elkanah her husband to her, Hannah, why weepest thou? and why eatest thou not? and why is thy heart grieved? am not I better to thee than ten sons?
>
> —1 Samuel 1:4–8

One key phrase in this passage of scripture is that "*the Lord had shut up her womb.*" This is essential to understand because anything the Lord shuts up, He can also open up. Yes, Hannah's natural womb had been shut up, but the womb of her mind and heart would not be shut up. For even though Peninnah had been fulfilling the role of providing male heirs for the household, Hannah had not settled within her mind that she would not have seed. Her mind was still fertile.

Even when her husband proclaimed that his love was so strong toward her that it was better than having ten sons, Hannah was not satisfied. She wept, yet in her sorrow she still had focus. Hannah took her plea and her tears to the house of the Lord.

Though it was commonly believed that having no seed was

a curse from God, Hannah still approached the place where God's presence was. Hannah, even in her "shut up" state, was not shut up from the presence of the Lord. Even though Eli the priest misunderstood her cries and moaning, God clearly understood. When Hannah had settled the issue with the Lord, she got up from that place of travail. When she arose, it was to a place of triumph.

> And she said, Let thine handmaid find grace in thy sight. So the woman went her way, and did eat, and her countenance was no more sad.
> —1 SAMUEL 1:18

The time of travail was over and the time of preparation had begun. Could it be that the eating of food was an indicator of faith and Hannah was preparing her natural body to be healthy and ready to nourish a growing fetus? In any case, it was not long before she conceived and brought forth Samuel. The Lord had remembered Hannah and her plea found a place of compassion within His heart. He reversed the charges on Hannah's physical womb and opened up that which had been previously closed.

Hannah gave birth to Samuel when the time was right. God's timing is always perfect. For the seed that came through Hannah was not just God's compassionate response to Hannah's pleas. It would also express the heart of God at a time when the earthly priesthood was in dire need of integrity. The birth of Samuel signaled a new era in the temple. The rearing of Samuel in the temple fulfilled God's desire to position a trustworthy man in the sacred office of an earthly priest.

The name "Samuel" means "asked of the Lord" or "heard of by God." Not only did Hannah ask for this child, but the Lord also asked for the child. Hannah was sensitive and wise enough to give this child back to the Lord when she brought him back to the temple after he had been weaned. God was well pleased with Hannah's fulfillment of the oath that she would give the child back to the Lord and this previously barren woman was then blessed with five more children.

We cannot outgive God. When we give to the service of the King, the King will return to us a King's reward. Samuel lived a righteous life and fulfilled the office of priest just as God would have him to do. Hannah's being "shut up" by the Lord was actually a way for God to prepare a godly man for the position of priest in His earthly temple. Hannah's seed was really God's seed.

Hence, Hannah's womb story offers encouragement for us to be honest with God, trust in His timing, and be confident that if it is His will He will use us to bring forth an honorable vessel to be used in His service.

ELISABETH'S WOMB-WONDERFUL STORY

> And they had no child, because that Elisabeth was barren, and they both were now well stricken in years....But the angel said unto him, Fear not, Zacharias: for thy prayer is heard; and thy wife Elisabeth shall bear thee a son, and thou shalt call his name John. And thou shalt have joy and gladness; and many shall rejoice at his birth. For he shall be great in the sight of the Lord, and shall drink neither wine nor strong drink; and he shall be filled with the Holy Ghost, even from his mother's womb.
> —LUKE 1:7, 13–15

The story surrounding the womb of Elisabeth is a tremendous one that clearly relates to us that every issue out of the womb is for the purpose of bringing God's plan for man to fruition. Here was an old couple, Zacharias and Elisabeth. These folks were righteous, which means that they lived a life that held them in right standing with God. Zacharias was of the eighth course of the priestly tribe of Abia, of which Aaron had been the high priest. Elisabeth was from the same priestly tribe and her name is actually the same name as the wife of the high priest Aaron.

This couple had lived a long life of faithfulness to God. Now God was about to be faithful to them. Elisabeth is described as being barren. Could it have been that she was being punished for some reason?

Again, we must pause here and recognize that when we walk uprightly before God and are true to Him, our barrenness is not about us but is about what God wants to do through us. Here, the very sincere challenge will be to trust God and trust that His ways will eventually bring understanding as to why you have no seed.

Even though their desire to have a child may have passed, God still shows up in His miraculous power. God's use of this elderly couple is a picture of the condition of the world at that particular time. Just as they were old and fruitless, the world was old and fruitless. It was not bringing forth the fruit of godliness. Just as Elisabeth's womb had deteriorated, such was the state of the world. Therefore as a sign of the times and of miraculous possibilities through Him, God took Elisabeth's womb and filled it with a child who would prepare the world for the Messiah Jesus Christ.

God sent a messenger to them to tell them that they had been chosen. In other words, they had been separated and called apart to be the parents of a separated man-child.

The world was in need of a light. However, this light was not just going to appear. Instead, because Jesus was and is a King, He was going to be announced much in the same way a person of earthly royalty would be announced when entering a room or visiting another country. In preparation of receiving royalty, the government hosting the king or queen may pave roads, fix street lights, prune trees, and shape hedges.

God would be using John the Baptist to prepare the world for the entrance of the King of kings and Lord of lords—Jesus the Christ. John would announce to the world that they must get themselves ready for the entrance of one much mightier than him.

God chose Zacharias and Elisabeth because of their priestly heritage and because they had led lives of separation unto God and of service to His people. Now they would be entrusted to bring forth a seed that was also separated for servitude in the mission of God. First of all, John the Baptist was separated unto purpose while he was in his mother's womb. For when Mary (who at this time was carrying in her womb the Lord Jesus) came into the presence of her cousin, Elisabeth (who had in her womb, John the Baptist), John leaped within Elisabeth's womb.

The father of John the Baptist had been told that John would be filled with the Holy Ghost, even from the womb. Up until then the Holy Spirit or Holy Ghost had fallen on man and then the presence of the Holy Spirit would lift. But John the Baptist's father was told that the Holy Ghost would not just rest upon John and lift, but the Holy Spirit would be within John even while he was in the womb.

John the Baptist's boldness would come from the indwelling presence of God. For the Holy Spirit is in the presence of God and is in direct partnership and relationship with Jesus and God. Thus, John the Baptist (while yet in the womb) was fully equipped and ready to carry out his duty.

John the Baptist, who came from parents who were separated by lineage and by lifestyle, was also separated unto God. He, too, was to not drink wine nor strong drink.

John was further different and separated from those of his time. He dressed in camels' hair and a leather girdle. He ate locusts and wild honey. He lived in the wilderness, separate from people and the common influences of the world.

John's separation was a form of preparation. It would qualify him to herald the One and to call men to separate themselves from the conditions of that present dark world. At the appropriate time, John welcomed people to hear his message that was radical enough to prepare the atmosphere for the most radical entrance of all time.

Therefore, Elisabeth's womb story is one of prepared glory. The fruit of her womb was honoured to be the forerunner, the announcer, and the forecaster of the Lord, Jesus Christ. Irony here presents itself, because Zacharias was unable to speak from the time he heard the message from the angel until his son was born. This was because he had spoken words of doubt about what the angel had told him. Therefore, the angel nullified the effect of Zacharias' doubt by shutting up his mouth until the miracle was complete. Now, instead of Elisabeth's womb being barren, the mouth of Zacharias was barren.

Zacharias' voice could be heard once John was born. Also, the voice of the heavenly Father could be heard once John the Baptist became the voice of God crying out in the wilderness, "Prepare ye the way of the Lord."

John's message was different from any message before his time. Even while he was still in his mother's womb, he was filled with the Holy Ghost. Indeed, there is something different when one is Holy Ghost-filled. Had he not been filled with the Holy Ghost, John would not have been qualified to talk about the One, Jesus Christ, who "shall baptize you with the Holy Ghost and with fire" (Luke 3:16). John received the Holy Ghost, but Jesus has the Holy Ghost with fire. It is this fire-propelled Holy Ghost that causes every Holy Ghost-filled person to want to witness to the world as John did, and say like he said, "I may baptize you with water, but what you really need is to be baptized with the Holy Ghost and with fire."

In spite of Zacharias's initial doubt, after his son was born his first words were those that were spoken to him by the angel. Rather than naming his son according to tradition, Zacharias named him what the angel had told him the child's name would be. By doing this, Zacharias set a fatherly example, for John would also speak forth that which he had been commissioned by God to speak.

Mary's
Womb–Wonderful Story

> And in the sixth month the angel Gabriel was sent from God unto a city of Galilee, named Nazareth, To a virgin espoused to a man whose name was Joseph, of the house of David; and the virgin's name was Mary. And the angel came in unto her, and said, Hail, thou that art highly favoured, the Lord is with thee: blessed art thou among women. And when she saw him, she was troubled at his saying, and cast in her mind what manner of salutation this should be. And the angel said unto her, Fear not, Mary: for thou hast found favour with God. And, behold, thou shalt conceive in thy womb, and bring forth a son, and shalt call his name JESUS. He shall be great, and shall be called the Son of the Highest: and the Lord God shall give unto him the throne of his father David: And he shall reign over the house of Jacob for ever; and of his kingdom there shall be no end. Then said Mary unto the angel, How shall this be, seeing I know not a man? And the angel answered and said unto her, The Holy Ghost shall come upon thee, and the power of the Highest shall overshadow thee: therefore also that holy thing which shall be born of thee shall be called the Son of God.

> —Luke 1:26–35

Perhaps this biblical account is the most surprising womb story of them all. For here we have an unsuspecting virgin girl being told that she will soon be pregnant with the Son of God! Mary was a proper vessel because her womb was sanctified and holy. She had maintained her virginity and was looking forward to presenting herself as a virgin to Joseph.

Upon the appearance and salutation of the angel Gabriel, Mary was troubled. The angel immediately put Mary at ease. The angel told her not to be fearful. God had found her to be worthy of His divine favor. This information was followed by the news of a lifetime, as the angel revealed the full content of his message. At this point Mary had no fear, but she did have a natural response. Mary wondered how this could be because she had never had sexual relations with a man. The angel then told her that what is about to happen would be a holy thing. The angel told Mary that the Holy Ghost would come upon her and the power of God would overshadow her to bring about the conception of a Holy Seed.

It is important to note here that this conception took place with the presence and permission of the Trinity—God the Father, God the Son, and God the Holy Spirit. This was an all-powerful pregnancy by an all-present and all-knowing God. The presence of the Father and the Holy Ghost makes perfect sense because Jesus Christ is the expressed image of the Father, who is all-holy and all-powerful, even as the Holy Spirit is. This conception was like no other. Rather than there being the earthly presence of a male, there was the heavenly presence of the Father and the Spirit. This pregnancy would not involve just two (a male and a female). It would involve four: the Father, the Son, the Holy Spirit, and the needed incubator—Mary's womb.

This news was also accompanied by "confirmation" when the angel of the Lord told Mary that her elderly cousin, Elisabeth, was also going to have a son. Surely if this shocking announcement concerning old Elisabeth and Zacharias were true, this other announcement would also come to pass. Both announcements were accurate indeed. When the angel told her that Elisabeth was pregnant, how far along Elisabeth was and the sex of the unborn child, Mary said "*be it unto me.*"

Perhaps this news was enough for Mary to decide to go and personally bare witness of Elisabeth's pregnancy. Mary obviously knew Elisabeth well enough to know that if Elizabeth had conceived a child in her old age, then Elisabeth's pregnancy must have also been a part of this divine plan of God.

> And Mary said, Behold the handmaid of the Lord; be it unto me according to thy word. And the angel departed from her. And Mary arose in those days, and went into the hill country with haste, into a city of Juda; And entered into the house of Zacharias, and saluted Elisabeth. And it came to pass, that, when Elisabeth heard the salutation of Mary, the babe leaped in her womb; and Elisabeth was filled with the Holy Ghost: And she spake out with a loud voice, and said, Blessed art thou among women, and blessed is the fruit of thy womb. And whence is this to me, that the mother of my Lord should come to me? For, lo, as soon as the voice of thy salutation sounded in mine ears, the babe leaped in my womb for joy. And blessed is she that believed: for there shall be a performance of those things which were told her from the Lord.
>
> —LUKE 1:38–45

Immediately upon Mary's arrival to see her, Elisabeth confirmed what the angel had told Mary even though Mary had not yet told her what the angel had said. Elisabeth hailed the mother of the Savior of the world and praised God for the fact that all that was spoken by God shall come to pass.

This account of Mary's womb lets us know that even an unsuspecting womb can be used for the glory of God. Being available and prepared is key to being involved with the plan of God. Mary's womb was prepared because it was sacred and sanctified. Today God is looking for sacred places and sanctified persons to carry out His will. Much like Mary's womb was prepared to house the body of the Savior, our spiritual wombs must be prepared to house the presence of the Spirit of the Savior of the world.

STUDY/DISCUSSION QUESTIONS

1. Do you think Rebekah's preferential treatment of Jacob affected his choices? How did this choice "train" Jacob as an infant, toddler, young boy, teen, young adult, and adult?

2. Why did God choose to use Jacob in spite of his being a "Mama's boy"?

3. In what way did the birth of Joseph bring hope to Rachel?

4. Have you ever been a "Joseph"? In what ways can favoritism seem more like a curse than a blessing?

5. Why is it important to keep some dreams to yourself?

6. In looking at the life of Samson, examine the fact that no matter how a mother brings up her child, the time will come when the choices made will be his or her own.

7. Do you think Samson's mother would have eaten the honey if she had known it was unclean? Why or why not?

8. What is the difference between natural strength and physical strength? When should either or both of these be relied upon?

9. In what ways can a bitter woman (like Ruth) be used to make a better woman (like Naomi)?

10. Why do you think God chose to use the life of Ruth and the womb of Naomi to bring forth His Son, Jesus Christ (out of that lineage)?

11. How was Naomi a successful mentor despite her seemingly unsuccessful and unfruitful past? Do you think Naomi's past was brought to bear when she gave instructions to Ruth?

12. Hannah promised Samuel to the Lord's service. Have we gone past the time where we can promise our children to the Lord's service?

13. At what times in your life have you given to God and subsequently He gave back to you over and over again?

14. Do you think there is a mentor relationship between Elisabeth and Mary?

15. Does God-given strength of a wife sometimes override the temporary doubt of a husband?

16. Why would it be important to watch the company you keep during a natural pregnancy and also during a spiritual pregnancy?

17. What struggles would Mary have faced had she lived in this twenty-first century?

18. What attributes did Mary possess that enabled her to successfully carry out the will of the heavenly Father in her life?

19. What rules would Mary have had for herself throughout her pregnancy? How may we use these same rules to nurture the dreams within our spiritual wombs?

PRAYER

Father in heaven, I want to thank You for how the Word shows us that You specialize in barren wombs. Father, You show us that there is nothing that is too hard for You. God, I give You my empty wombs and I place them in Your will and the perfect design You have for my life. Lord, I thank You that I am not a failure in You. You have placed within me an unseen purpose, but through faith I thank You that it shall be seen. Have Your way in my life. Use me to fill the world with miracles. In Jesus' name, I pray. Amen.

Chapter Seven

The Seven
Wombs in Existence

THE ORIGINAL OR
FIRST WOMB—THE MIND OF GOD

In the beginning God created the heaven and the earth.

—GENESIS 1:1

The original womb is the mind of God. Why? Because housed in the mind of God was and is everything that was ever to be in existence. For example—the universe, the heavens, and the earth. The power which God had to create from His mind, was His expressed thought. That is, God spoke it and it was! This is why God warns us in His Word of the power of the spoken word.

> Death and life are in the power of the tongue: and they that love it shall eat the fruit thereof.
> —PROVERBS 18:21

Obviously then, we should refrain from speaking words of doubt, despair, and depression. For, just like our heavenly Father, our words come alive and manifest. Some refer to this divine ability as a self-fulfilling prophecy. Imagine a world where the Christians only spoke the Bible. That is, a world where Christians speak forth life and of impossibilities becoming possibilities. Faith speaks not of what seems to be, but of what shall be according to the divine will of the heavenly Father. Just as God can create, He has given His seed the ability to create.

There are two words for the term *create*:

The first word is *Asa*.

> ASA—means to create something out of something else. This is like making a cake out of its ingredients. This is like giving a child paper and crayons and watching him draw a picture of a flower, cat, or dog.

The second word is *Bara*.

> BARA—means to create out of nothing. Only God can do this. There was a void, emptiness, or a vacuum and then God created everything. No one on this earth can create something from nothing. Even inventors work with something that is already in existence. Even when a "new discovery" is made, God is permitting what was covered to be uncovered.

Bara occurred when God created the universe from His

mind. At this point the first womb has given birth to the next womb.

THE SECOND
WOMB—THE UNIVERSE

> And the earth was without form, and void; and darkness was upon the face of the deep. And the Spirit of God moved upon the face of the waters.
> —GENESIS 1:2

The universe is the second womb. This universe contains everything that man knows and man does not know. The components of any of man's inventions since the earliest days had already been provided in the universe. Also, every planet in the universe that is yet to be investigated or studied by scientists, is already well-known by its Creator—God.

THE THIRD WOMB—THE EARTH

The universe is filled with waters. Out of the waters of this womb, Earth was birthed. When God created the earth, He actually created another womb. For this Earth is filled with potential. In the early days of the life of the earth, the environment was perfect for growth—like an enclosed greenhouse. Rather than rain providing water needed for growth, a mist went up each day and watered the whole ground.

Earth was self-sufficient because it reflected Him. Before man entered in the earth, there was absolutely no sin, and therefore the whole earth operated in perfection. However, when man sinned, sin stained this perfect place and from that time onward it had to be "taken care of." Since the first sin, the earth has depleted itself and the earth has become less and less perfect.

> And God called the dry land Earth; and the gathering
> together of the waters called he Seas: and God saw
> that it was good. And God said, Let the earth bring
> forth grass, the herb yielding seed, and the fruit tree
> yielding fruit after his kind, whose seed is in itself,
> upon the earth: and it was so. And the earth brought
> forth grass, and herb yielding seed after his kind, and
> the tree yielding fruit, whose seed was in itself, after
> his kind: and God saw that it was good.
>
> —GENESIS 1:10–12

Out of this womb, earth, God created or gave birth to man-kind. I say "gave birth to" because it came from His womb or His mind. Man came from the earth, which came from the universe, which came from God.

Mankind is certainly the image of God. One item of evidence of the fact that mankind is in the image of God is that like God, the inventor of anything can only give out what is already stored in their mind. Another exhibit of evidence is that like our heavenly Father, we are tripartied. We are spirit, soul, and body. When we view each other, we are looking at godly beings. We are not the Holy Spirit or immortal bodies or even perfected souls, but we are the image of our Father and so we must strive to be as He is. We will not reach this perfected state on the earth, but when Jesus returns, every person who has lived according to His precepts and example will be perfected just as He is. That is, every person will be rewarded with a returning to our original condition of perfection. This is the perfection that was before sin entered and stained the world.

> For this corruptible must put on incorruption, and
> this mortal must put on immortality. So when this
> corruptible shall have put on incorruption, and this
> mortal shall have put on immortality, then shall be

brought to pass the saying that is written, Death is swallowed up in victory.

—1 CORINTHIANS 15:53–54

Beloved, now are we the sons of God, and it doth not yet appear what we shall be: but we know that, when he shall appear, we shall be like him; for we shall see him as he is.

—1 JOHN 3:2

And the LORD God formed man of the dust of the ground, and breathed into his nostrils the breath of life; and man became a living soul.

—GENESIS 2:7

And God made the beast of the earth after his kind, and cattle after their kind, and every thing that creep-eth upon the earth after his kind: and God saw that it was good. And God said, Let us make man in our image, after our likeness: and let them have domin-ion over the fish of the sea, and over the fowl of the air, and over the cattle, and over all the earth, and over every creeping thing that creepeth upon the earth. So God created man in his own image, in the image of God created he him; male and female cre-ated he them.

—GENESIS 1:25–27

When God created mankind out of the womb of the world, man was made from the dust of the ground, which came from the dust in the universe, which came from the dust which was in the very being and mind of God.

God has placed His creation on the earth to reflect His very character. Everything we need to do this has already been supplied by God. Certainly, God would not put us on the earth and not give us what is needed to be complete and whole in everything. Since mankind was formed from the earth, humans feed from those things which have been supplied by the earth through the food chain.

THE FOURTH WOMB—ADAM

> And the LORD God caused a deep sleep to fall upon Adam, and he slept: and he took one of his ribs, and closed up the flesh instead thereof; And the rib, which the LORD God had taken from man, made he a woman, and brought her unto the man. And Adam said, This is now bone of my bones, and flesh of my flesh: she shall be called Woman, because she was taken out of Man.
>
> —GENESIS 2:21–23

Out of Adam's womb God created Eve. This act of God was the first major surgery ever performed. God administered a supernatural anesthesia that caused Adam to fall asleep. God then opened up His creation, took information out of His creation, and then closed His creation back up. The surgery was complete and it was successful.

When God took out one of Adam's ribs this demonstrated a couple of things. First, Adam's rib contained his blood cells and therefore God removed the necessary information for making another person. Secondly, Adam would have a natural affinity for this new creation because it came out of him. Thirdly, because Adam had come from the earth which had come from the universe which had come from the mind of God, this new man (called woman) also came from the mind of God. The essence of this whole process is that everything that is now being created has originated from the ultimate Source, which is God.

At this time, Adam had already spent time existing with and naming the animals and plants. This new being was himself with a major difference, this new "him" had a womb.

This woman, his wife, would now be a help meet fitly made for him.

It must be noted here that since a rib was removed from Adam, this meant that he was no longer complete, for he was missing his rib. Therefore, Adam now was made complete when he embraced his rib and became united with her in marriage. This speaks to the institution of marriage and how sacred it is that a man and a woman combine. A woman completes a man. No matter how many man-made laws are enacted or approved, God established in the beginning that a woman belongs with her man. For a man and a man can never bring forth out of the natural, physical womb, and the female and the female can never bring forth out of their natural womb, without the genetic inclusion of the male's DNA. The bottom line is that in order for life to continue, there must be the union of male and female.

THE FIFTH WOMB—EVE

And Adam called his wife's name Eve; because she was the mother of all living.

—GENESIS 3:20

Adam calls this woman who had come from him a befitting name. She is called Eve, which indicates her purpose, for she is the mother of all living. Because Eve was the first of the living to give birth, we all came from the womb of Eve. Never again would a man be put to sleep to bring forth life. From then on, it would be the natural womb within the body of the female that would carry the fetus and bring forth new life.

Eve was also a part of a perfect environment—at least for a brief season. However, this utopia was destroyed when the serpent tempted Eve to eat of the forbidden fruit. The food chain was in operation as this fruit was passed on to Adam, and he ate what his woman had offered him. In this very moment everything on the earth changed for the worse. For now the couple's eyes were opened to the evil that exists. Now they would have to fight for what had previously been given to them. That is, they would have to fight for peace, for the presence of God, and for the fulfillment of their purpose on Earth.

At this point God had to step in and administer consequences for their actions. So Adam had to work and take responsibility for the woman and their children that would be born. Eve had to now bear children in pain and she had to be submissive to her husband. These severe consequences continue to this day.

Every time a woman gives birth, she is reminded of the sin of mother Eve. This is also why it can be said that even at birth, the baby is sinful. Also because the sin nature has been inherited from Adam and Eve, at birth every baby carries the curse of sin and is therefore sinful. The result of this is that we still have to struggle against our sinful nature even though we have submitted our wills to the lordship of Jesus Christ. Now, we must fight daily to avoid sin and to become more like Jesus.

The Sixth Womb— Your Womb—Our Natural Womb

> So God created man in his own image, in the image of God created he him; male and female created he them. And God blessed them, and God said unto them, Be fruitful, and multiply, and replenish the earth, and subdue it: and have dominion over the fish of the sea, and over the fowl of the air, and over every living thing that moveth upon the earth.
> —Genesis 1:27–28

Lo, children are an heritage of the LORD: and the fruit of the womb is his reward. As arrows are in the hand of a mighty man; so are children of the youth. Happy is the man that hath his quiver full of them: they shall not be ashamed, but they shall speak with the enemies in the gate.

—PSALM 127:3

The blessing of the LORD, it maketh rich, and he addeth no sorrow with it.

—PROVERBS 10:22

Even after the fall of Adam and Eve, God honored the blessing which He had bestowed upon them when He told them to be "fruitful and multiply." The difference now was that multiplication and provision would be painful. Furthermore, the devil received vital and critical information in Genesis 3:15, when God said to him, "And I will put enmity between thee and the woman, and between thy seed and her seed; it shall bruise thy head, and thou shalt bruise his heel." This Scripture verse has been the impetus for the devil's lust for people to be destroyed. For it is one thing to bruise a heel, for with a bruised heel, one can still limp and move on. However, a bruised head is deadly. The head is what houses the mind. It also suggest authority.

Since the seed of the woman was to bruise, injure, deform, or disfigure the enemy's head, the devil has set out to destroy the seed:

- Before it incubates or grows.

- Before it sees the light of day, and begins to walk in its purpose and destiny.

- Before the map that God has already made for this child will never be seen or carried out.

The ultimate aim and objective of Satan is to see that God's Word does not become manifest. For when these words are manifest, it will mean that he (the devil) has been destroyed for eternity. Therefore from the time of the Garden of Eden until this very day, Satan has continued to go after the womb of mankind. As a matter of fact as long as time continues, there is an increase in the deceptive ways the enemy of God devises to either kill the seed of the woman before it makes it out of the womb, or to have the seed of the woman destroyed before it reaches its greatest potential in life.

It used to be that killing the seed of a woman was shameful. Unfortunately and sadly, undesired pregnancies often ended in backstreet abortions. We must understand that just as God always has a "ram in the thicket," Satan also always has a man in the backstreet who is willing to perform his dirty work. The pitiful thing is that it is often done under the guise of caring for the female who is caught up in this trap. Today, things have changed somewhat. For no longer are the abortion rooms located in places of obscurity, but they are found in the best hospitals and clinics around the world. No longer do most of the women cringe in shame. Instead, many women voice that it is their body and they have a right to do to it as they desire. It used to be that females tried to quiet the guilt of their own inner voice by aborting the fetus before it looked human. Now there are those who abort the fetus no matter what stage of growth it is in. The current legislation on the "rights" of women have no concerns about the rights of God's holy Word, much less the rights of the unborn child.

Contraceptive methods are in existence to prevent pregnancy. Yet, the abortion clinics of the world have become many people's choice for "birth control." We must understand that every unseen, unborn, unconcieved, and unthought of child has already been known by God. Remember, it began in the womb of His mind. Every time that particular sperm unites with that particular egg, God already has pre-knowledge of it. God knows the potential of that union because He has already sanctioned its life and its life plan. To destroy that which God has already allowed and planned for, is to strike a blow at the creativity and omniscience of God. Satan is making an allout effort to "get back" at God's pronouncement of damnation upon him by limiting the effectiveness of God's creation. Satan delights in anything that annihilates the fruit of God's womb.

The fact is, Satan cannot stand God or His image, and therefore he cannot stand to see them born. Satan cannot stand to see life. The Bible tells us in John 10:10 that, "The thief cometh not, but for to steal, and to kill, and to destroy: I am come that they might have life, and that they might have it more abundantly." Whatever the plan of Satan is, Jesus has already reversed the curse. Even though Satan desires to steal, kill, and destroy, God has instituted the ultimate reversal of this through His redemptive plan for mankind.

Many women suffer today because they made a decision to have an abortion. Even if this tragedy happened years or even decades ago, feelings of shame and guilt linger, in some cases as though it had happened only yesterday. Because it is so natural for a woman to give life, the choice made years earlier will haunt the woman as she matures and realizes the gravity of what she did. By God's grace and mercy, though, many of these women find forgiveness and peace in Christ Jesus.

Tragedy is heaped upon tragedy when a woman becomes sterile after going through a dramatic abortion. The woman is often devastated when she feels ready to have a family, but this past decision to abort comes back like the headlight of a speeding freight train. When this happens, the devil has stolen life from the woman, killed the life from within the woman, and impeded her from bringing forth life in the future. Along with this, the tissue remnants of an aborted baby are discarded in conditions that are not even due an animal.

It is important that when we express the mercy and

understanding we need to give to any woman experiencing an unwanted pregnancy, we must not condone or recommend a planned abortion. Condoning a plan to kill life is the same as condoning a man's plan to murder someone and doing nothing to stop it.

What we do not and cannot understand about an unwanted pregnancy can never give us permission to kill the image of God. The union that resulted in the fertilized egg has already been established and allowed in God's mind.

THE SEVENTH WOMB—OUR OTHER WOMB—OUR SPIRITUAL WOMB

Let this mind be in you, which was also in Christ Jesus.

—PHILIPPIANS 2:5

But as it is written, Eye hath not seen, nor ear heard, neither have entered into the heart of man, the things which God hath prepared for them that love him. But God hath revealed them unto us by his Spirit: for the Spirit searcheth all things, yea, the deep things of God. For what man knoweth the things of a man, save the spirit of man which is in him? even so the things of God knoweth no man, but the Spirit of God. Now we have received, not the spirit of the world, but the spirit which is of God; that we might know the things that are freely given to us of God. Which things also we speak, not in the words which man's wisdom teacheth, but which the Holy Ghost teacheth; comparing spiritual things with spiritual. But the natural man receiveth not the things of the Spirit of God: for they are foolishness unto him: neither can he know them, because they are spiritually discerned. But he that is spiritual judgeth all things, yet he himself is judged of no man. For who hath known the mind of the Lord, that he may instruct him? But we have the mind of Christ.

—1 CORINTHIANS 2:9–16

Whether male or female, every living person has a spiritual womb. Why? Because, like our Father, the gift of creativity and the desire to "bring forth" have been housed in our minds. Just as God brought forth all that is, mankind is not satisfied in living unless he has truly fulfilled his potential by also bringing forth all that is in his mind.

A peaceful mind indicates that those things which they have perceived and then conceived in their spiritual womb (their mind) is now manifest. That is, the idea or image or invention is no longer housed safely in the womb of the mind, but now can be seen by all. We must keep in focus that the spiritual baby (the vision within you) cannot remain in you forever and keep on living. *It must come forth!* Those things which God allows men to see with their minds are like that fetus in the womb that can be seen on the ultrasound. Just like the baby in the natural womb, those things in the spiritual womb of the mind will never be fully appreciated and admired until they are seen among all.

Each of us is accountable to God for the creativity He has placed within us. (This principle is similar to the one in the parable of the talents we read about in Matthew 25.) For God decided before the foundation of time, to place certain creative ideas within the minds of mankind. Therefore God is expecting to see these ideas come forth. God desires to see the man or woman's womb bring forth the vision so that He might say, "Well done, thou good and faithful servant" (Matt. 25:21).

The enemy works contrary to this plan. He desires that we stifle creativity, that we suffocate new ideas and that we silence our imagination. Satan loves it when we discourage each other from attaining to great heights in Christ Jesus. Satan loves it when we try to discourage those who continue to climb their pre-ordained ladder of success. When we are successful in this, we are spiritual abortionists, killing the dreams of our brothers and sisters in Christ!

For this reason, we must take great care to not offend others with abortion pills that we may drop into the the spiritual wombs housing their visions. We must take great care to encourage rather than discourage. Encouragement is so very powerful. Like Barnabas, we must build bridges rather than tear them down. We must look for the good in everyone, and then nurture this good. For it is out of this goodness that God, our heavenly Father, will be glorified.

God specializes in unity. Satan, on the other hand, specializes in bringing division. Where there is unity, the vision of the church pastor will be seen to be flourishing, the vision of the church member will be seen flourishing, and the vision of all will be appreciated and esteemed. Jesus' final plea and prayer was for the unity of the church. Jesus occupied His final moments of intercessory prayer by speaking to the Father on our behalf for the weapon of unity. Our enemy, Satan, works to divide us and one of the best ways to counteract his schemes is to speak blessing over and intercede for our brothers and sisters in Christ. As Christians, corporately and individually, seek the mind of God and begin to worship Him in spirit and in truth, the church body will experience growth and development as never before.

Jesus, our ultimate example, looked for good and productivity in the most hated of all man. Why would Jesus invest time with hated tax collectors, despised Pharisees, and the shunned sick? Jesus understood that because even these men originated from the womb of God, goodness was in them. Jesus spent time with these men and many of them changed and became who their heavenly Father made them to be. These men were no longer conformed to the world's way of living, but their minds became transformed and renewed (made again as in the beginning). This happened when Jesus recognized these men and women's spiritual wombs.

Because of the forces at work to kill what is within your womb, it is most crucial that you are careful about who knows that you are spiritually pregnant. For there are those who have not grasped the fact that God desires spiritual children. Some Christians really do not understand that when their fellow brother or sister is "inspired" to bring forth a vision, this is a spiritual pregnancy that must be protected. It is important for this new vision to be welcomed like we would a new baby into our very own families. This welcoming is necessary because the church family is responsible for feeding the vision and helping it grow. In summation, once the vision comes forth from the spiritual womb, it is to be celebrated and embraced by all—it takes a village to raise a vision.

God has given every person a spiritual womb. However, we must be close enough in our relationship with God for Him to reveal to us what it is. This is important because those who know their specific vision will know that they are unique and that no one in the body of Christ can bring forth fruit that is identical to theirs. In other words, there is no spiritual cloning in the house of God. What God has given to one is not totally identical to what He has given to another. Instead of duplicating, He multiplies. Every seed or multiplication that comes forth is a one-of-a-kind creation. In summation, the DNA of your spiritual womb will never match up to any one else's.

Here are some ways to protect your spiritual womb.

- *Watch what you eat.* Feed only on the Word of God for direct nourishment. Anything that is contrary to the Word of God will result in infection and disease. Any allowance of that which is not spiritually healthful to enter into your spiritual life may result in a spiritual miscarriage.

- *Avoid stress.* Your environment is so very important as you carry the spiritual baby within your spiritual womb. Watch where you go and who you travel with. Outward stressful conditions will eventually lead to inward damage to the unique seed you are carrying.

- *Walk carefully.* The further along you are in the spiritual pregnancy or the closer you are to giving birth, the more carefully you must spiritually walk. Stay focused in the Word of God. Walk in the fruit of the Spirit. Walk continually as a peacemaker. Walk away from dangerous places. Be careful where you take your precious unborn vision. Your seed is most important.

- *Have consistent checkups.* Go to your doctor, or might I say to your pastor or spiritual leader. Let your leader know how things are progressing in your spiritual pregnancy. Check yourself in the mirror of the Word of God. Check yourself as the taught and preached Word is delivered. Check your heart rate. Know how to express what you are feeling instead of bottling up your feelings. Internalizing feelings will not be good for your spiritual baby.

- *Take those vitamins.* Although vitamins are sometimes difficult to swallow, they are necessary. Vitamins are profound revelations of God's Word or words of correction from a respected leader. Take the "vitamin" even though it tastes terrible. It really will do your body and your spiritual baby good.

The fulfillment of your destiny, the quality of your life, and the quality of the life of those around you depends upon your doing all this and more to nourish and protect your spiritual pregnancy. Whether it is a natural baby or a spiritual one that is cut off, this generation and those to come will suffer the consequences of the loss. The life within us is much too precious for us to harm the visions of others or our own.

STUDY/DISCUSSION QUESTIONS

1. How can faith that God is all-sufficient help us to do His will here on the earth?

2. How is it that all medicine and medication is a by-product of the earth?

3. Why does the enemy strategize to destroy Adam's seed?

4. What attributes do women have that could be used to cause a man do what he ought not to do?

5. In what ways does the modern-day fight for women's rights contradict God's plan and purpose for all life? Is this contradiction limited to home life?

6. Are there limits as to what a "right to life" advocate should do in supporting God's purpose of life?

7. What measures will a woman take to protect her physical womb during pregnancy? Is it important to take these kinds of measures to protect the spiritual womb?

PRAYER

Father, I thank You because I know that You have equipped us to bring forth life and that more abundantly. Lord, I ask that as I pursue purpose and destiny that You will cause my spiritual womb to bring forth every dream and every vision which You have placed within it. Thank You for placing within each of us a part of You. God, I understand that there is perfection within us. For this, I proclaim Your name and give You the glory for all that You have done and all that You will do. In Jesus' name, I pray. Amen.

Chapter Eight

Rejection Stories of the Womb

Hannah's Rejection Story

SATAN WOULD RATHER you be barren than bring forth fruit. For in the beginning, God's first blessing and command to mankind was to be fruitful and multiply. In the Old Testament it was a curse to be barren. This is why Hannah had a difficult time in 1 Samuel 1:8 which says, "Then said Elkanah her husband to her, Hannah, why weepest thou? and why eatest thou not? and why is thy heart grieved? am not I better to thee than ten sons?"

During the time of the Old Covenant (Old Testament), the fruitfulness of the womb was a sign that the Lord was pleased with you and that you were blessed. Thus, the contrary was also considered true. Therefore, Hannah had to tell her husband, "Listen, I love you dearly, but you cannot imagine the value of a son to me. Even you cannot reverse the fact that because I am barren, I am cursed." My paraphrase here shows that Hannah's despair could not be stopped as long as her barrenness remained.

> The grave; and the barren womb; the earth that is not filled with water; and the fire that saith not, It is enough.
> —PROVERBS 30:16

The verse in Proverbs 30:16 is so very potent. For it classifies the barren womb alongside other extreme examples of things that can in no way make one happy. In other words, what can one do to satisfy a barren womb? Nothing! Absolutely nothing. For the woman who cannot give birth never stops grieving. The woman who cannot give birth continually feels empty. The woman who cannot give birth will continually burn with a passion to have what she is incapable of having. As a matter of fact, if possible, a woman will spend her last dime to accomplish the goal of becoming a mother.

This is why the ending of Hannah's story of barrenness brings us such a tremendous sigh of relief. God heard her desperate cry and opened up her womb. Then just like only God can do, He blessed her more than she could ever have hoped for or dreamed of. For her womb not only opened up and brought forth one child, Samuel, but she lived to have five more children.

LEAH'S REJECTION STORY

Another insightful biblical passage where God opens a barren womb is the story of Leah. In this account we see that when the love of her husband would not be manifested, God eventually consumed Leah's love for her husband into a love and a passion for her children. While it is true that this did not happen overnight, eventually over time Leah did fall in love with the fact that God had opened up her womb, over and over and over again.

> And when the LORD saw that Leah was hated, he opened her womb: but Rachel was barren.
>
> —GENESIS 29:31

> And she conceived again, and bare a son: and she said, Now will I praise the LORD: therefore she called his name Judah; and left bearing.
>
> —GENESIS 29:35

The account involving Jacob, Leah, and Rachel is quite the story. Here we find certain elements running continuously through the entire account. There is love, hate, deceit, conspiracy, jealousy, envy, despondency, and anger. If you are looking for a "talk show" atmosphere storyline, here it is. Nevertheless, this story presents itself as one of the most wonderful teaching tools available to the Christian today.

I believe an undercurrent or underlying theme of Leah's story is that we must not put our faith and trust in men, for indeed the arms of flesh will fail. For how many times had Jacob held Leah in his arms as he made love to her? Yet these same arms held another close to his heart. Even though Leah was able to conceive from out of her natural womb, she saw herself as infertile when it came to giving birth to her husband's love for her.

Perhaps we must take into great account that Leah gained the bed of Jacob first, rather than gaining his heart first. For Jacob married Leah under the misconception that she was her younger sister, Rachel. For in those days the bride was heavily veiled and Jacob was not able to see the specific physical features of his bride until the light of the next day and the lifting of the veil. The bottom line was that Jacob had been tricked.

Because we have already reviewed Jacob's background of plotting and trickery to get his brother Esau's inheritance, it is easy to deduce that he was reaping his own seed of trickery that he had planted years earlier. Jacob's womb brought forth fruit of deception earlier in life and then came back to haunt him later.

This story of Leah has some blanks in it, and so this allows us to discuss some possibilities of why the story turned out the way it did. For example, we never hear about Leah's opinion of marrying Jacob. We do know that the father of Leah and Rachel justified his deception by referring to the traditions of his country. The father of these two sisters said it was not right for the younger sister to marry before the older sister. Jacob was honorable in this situation and fulfilled Leah's week of marriage. Could it be that Jacob had some pity toward Leah? Could it be that Jacob understood it was not Leah's choice, but it was the Father's choice? In any case, Jacob did have sexual relations with her. Whether Jacob had pity on her or actually cared for her, we cannot be sure. Although the biblical account indicates that Jacob never did love Leah as he did love Rachel, he did choose to be buried next to Leah.

An interesting point to note here is that men and women view sexual intimacy in very different lights. Jacob had no problem lying with Leah even though he loved Rachel. On the other hand, Leah hoped that Jacob would grow to love her when she had sex with him. This thought pattern went even further when Leah began to think that the fruitfulness of her physical womb might be the key to opening up Jacob's heart toward her and veering it away from her younger sister. For when God had seen that she was hated, He had opened up her womb. Our examination of Leah and Jacob's relationship is an illustration of the fact that men and women do see sexual intimacy very differently.

Leah may not have been needed in Jacob's plans, but Leah

was a critical part in the plan of God. Therefore the opening of Leah's womb was critical to God. Why? Because there were some issues that needed to come forth out of Leah. Yes, out of a despised womb would come forth a nation whose God is the Lord. Out of Leah's despised womb would come forth a tribe that would usher in Jesus, the Lord and Saviour of the world. This reminds us to be careful of those whom we reject, for it could be that this will be the person God will use in very unexpected and mighty ways.

It took Leah quite a while to learn the value of her womb. At first her focus was on Jacob. Each time she conceived and then gave birth, she was aiming to gain Jacob's acceptance. Leah did not realize that she already had the acceptance of Jehovah Jireh—God, our Provider. So when Leah gave birth to her first son, she named him Reuben and her thoughts were that God has seen her affliction of not having her husband's love. Unfortunately for Leah, child number one did not change her state of affliction, for Jacob still did not love her.

Child number two was named Simeon, and once again her focus was on her affliction and her hope that her second son would cause Jacob to love her. Again, he did not love her. As Leah gives birth to her third son, it is in the midst of some serious thoughts of reality for Leah. Before Leah gave birth to her third child, she admits a fact that she had been avoiding. Leah admits that she is hated. What a cruel reality for a wife and mother to admit. Yet Leah erroneously believes that with the birth of a third son her husband's hatred for her will turn into love.

The situation here is very intense. Surely, emotions are running extremely high because Leah, who is hated and realizes it, is bringing forth life out of her womb. Also, Jacob, who loves Rachel, keeps on having sexual relations with Leah, resulting in one pregnancy after the other. Then there is Rachel, who is dearly loved and treasured by Jacob, but is standing by and watching all of the babies being born by

Leah. On the one hand, Leah keeps having babies but does not have the love of the man who is fathering her children. While on the other hand, Rachel has the love of her husband, but no fruit of her womb.

Something has changed when Leah gives birth to her fourth son, Judah. This time Leah's focus is not on gaining the love of Jacob. This time Leah realizes that she is loved by God. This time she has lifted her gaze and is now focused on praising God. Now she realizes that God has been there for her all of this time when He was blessing her with children by Jacob. God had looked upon her lowly estate and lifted her to a high place: a place of praising Him. Therefore, this newest son reflected Leah's new and improved condition. Now at the time when Leah could praise God, her son is given the name "Judah," which means "to give praise."

Once Leah had reached this momentous place of revelation concerning God's precious love toward her, her actions changed. For in that same verse, Genesis 29:35, we are told that Leah "left childbearing." This is powerful. Leah was no longer trying to secure Jacob's love by giving him children. Leah had reached a new place where she was more grateful for the love of God that had caused her to be able to have children and experience the precious love of children toward their mother. Now Leah could stop having children. She no longer needed to have children for the same reasons as before. So rather than trying to prove Jacob's love for her or trying to win Jacob's love away from her sister, Leah was satisfied in the love of God. In doing so, Leah even gave her maid Zilphah to bear children on her behalf.

Not only had Leah mentally left from childbearing, but her physical body had stopped bringing forth more seed. However, one more time we will see God's hand of favor with Leah's womb. For one day when Leah's son, Reuben, had worked in the fields and brought home his profit (mandrakes) to his mother, Rachel demanded the mandrakes from Leah. What a horrible scene this must have been! Anger and hurt welled up within Leah as she could not understand why Rachel would not only want her husband, but now Rachel wanted the very rewards that her son had labored for. Enough was enough! Rachel bargained with Leah on this day. This bargaining is very similar to the bargaining that had occurred between Jacob and Esau as recorded in Genesis 25:31. For on this day, Rachel told Leah that she would let Leah lay with Jacob and this would be payment for her retrieving the mandrakes for Reuben. Wow! What a predicament Leah was placed in.

Again, God rewarded Leah (who had left childbearing) by opening up her womb—yet again. This son was called Issachar, and his name means "to know the times and the seasons." Surely, when Leah bore this son, she knew that she had controlled the timing of this opportunity for conception. Leah was once again in a fruitful season, but this time it was with the full knowledge that Jacob did not love her. Leah went on to bear a sixth son named Zebulum, which means "security."

Leah now knew that no matter what happened, Jacob would not leave his sons or his first wife. Leah also went on to have a daughter named Dinah. Perhaps at this point and time, the significance of mentioning the birth of a daughter represents that Leah was now very sure and comfortable in herself as a mother and wife. For now even having a daughter was considered a blessing even though the daughter did not carry the financial value or traditional benefit that a male heir would have provided. At this point, Leah was content. She was content enough to enjoy her children now that she realized that God was the One who had blessed her over and over again.

When our wombs (natural or spiritual) have been blessed to bring forth life, there is an overwhelming feeling of satisfaction, and even more so when we recognize that it has not come through our own actions or ambitions. Leah finally understood that to have the love of God is a far greater gift than to have the love of man. When we can appreciate that God has opened our womb and blessed our womb, then we can be content and continually praise God for His expressions of His love for us.

MOSES' REJECTION STORY: WHEN THE BLESSING OF THE WOMB IS ABORTED

And the LORD spake unto Moses that selfsame day, saying, Get thee up into this mountain Abarim, unto mount Nebo, which is in the land of Moab, that is over against Jericho; and behold the land of Canaan, which I give unto the children of Israel for a possession: And die in the mount whither thou goest up, and be gathered unto thy people; as Aaron thy brother died in mount Hor, and was gathered unto his people: Because ye trespassed against me among the children of Israel at the waters of Meribah-Kadesh, in the wilderness of Zin; because ye sanctified me not in the midst of the children of Israel. Yet thou shalt see the land before thee; but thou shalt not go thither unto the land which I give the children of Israel.
—DEUTERONOMY 32:48–52

The story of Moses and his call to deliver the people of God out of the land of bondage is one filled with many peaks and valleys. For from chapter to chapter we are given the image of a conquering Moses and then a faltering Moses. Even from his youth, Moses was very much affected by the actions of others. Recall that when Moses saw one of his fellow Israelites being struck, he murdered an Egyptian man. That day forever changed the direction his life would take.

From the very beginning, the relationship between Moses and God's people was all about deliverance. In this case, Egypt is a figurative womb. God's people have been incubated in a place of bondage. Here, they have grown in strength and in might. However, as with the case of anything in a womb, when it has reached its maximum time of incubation, it is time for deliverance. Remaining in the womb of Egypt beyond the timing of God would have meant sure death for this nation.

Therefore, at the appointed time God sent a man into Egypt to demand Pharaoh let the children of Israel go free. Pharaoh was not willing to release God's people into their purpose and destiny. Pharaoh preferred that they work his land rather than enter their own promised land. The unreleased potential in the womb had to be set free so that the vision or dream would not die. God brought about many plagues to disturb the environment of the womb (the land of Egypt). Instead of the land of Egypt being at peace, it became a place of torment. Instead of the Egyptians having workers who were content with being under their control, they had workers who were beginning to look beyond their place of captivity and believe there had to be a better place for them.

Moses was the obstetrician-gynecologist whose hands would safely catch, hold, and then carry God's people to safety. This journey to the Promised Land was not easy, because after they left the womb of captivity in Egypt, the Israelites faced another womb. This was a harsh womb of nature called the wilderness. This wilderness seemed to last forever. Indeed what could have been a four-day journey ended up taking forty years. The long time period in this womb was the result of the fact that although the Israelites had left one womb, they still carried the attitude of that old environment and this interfered with their growth process and progress in the new womb that would bring them into the land that had been promised to them.

The wilderness was a testing womb. It tested and revealed their temperament and whether the people loved God or loved the idea of being free to do whatever they desired. As they wandered in the wilderness, God was breaking their independent spirit and purging their destructive ways. He used hunger, thirst, and time to determine that although the people had left the womb of Egypt, they still had much to learn in order to inherit a new awaiting womb—the Promised Land of Canaan. There was no way that God could allow them to bring their present mindset into the Promised Land. This people had to be changed and Moses was put in charge of changing them.

When the Israelites complained about not having food, it was Moses that spoke on their behalf. When the people were thirsty, it was Moses who again spoke on their behalf and caused God to rescue them. While in the wilderness, God's people were constantly dissatisfied. They were always rebelling and complaining. This is seen especially when Moses went to Mount Sinai to receive the Ten Commandments from the Lord. By the time Moses had returned, the people had rebelled. They had made a molten calf and were worshipping it. At this sight, Moses threw down the tablets of stone and broke that which the Lord God had made. At one point in the wilderness, Moses disobeyed God by striking a rock when God had told him to speak to the rock. It was the chiding of the people that had caused Moses to react in a negative way.

Essentially, Moses never gained full control of his temper. This led to his losing out on entering into the womb of the Promised Land of Canaan. God allowed him to see the land from the vantage point of Mount Nebo. It is as if Mount Nebo became a womb from which Moses was almost delivered. Sadly, even his bones never made it into the womb of the Promised Land of Canaan. This is such a sad end for a man whom the Lord knew "face to face." Moses had allowed his own reactions to the trespasses of the people of Israel to hinder him from completing the mission which had been delivered into his hands. This serves as a reminder that even when God has made a vision or dream to come forth from the spiritual womb, it is very possible for outside forces to abort the contents of the womb. Ultimately, Moses rejected wisdom and made decisions based on his emotional responses to the actions of foolish people. This resulted in his loss of the very thing that he had longed for. For while the people rejected Moses' counsel, Moses was unable to control his own sinful nature that had manifested early in his life when he lost his temper, killed the Egyptian, and was forced to flee for his life. Even though Moses had constantly reminded the people of God's faithfulness, his angry response to their unfaithfulness resulted in his own transgression against his God. God did not overlook this trespass, and the vision of Moses' heart was not fulfilled.

STUDY/DISCUSSION QUESTIONS

1. What are the dangers of remaining in a state of rejection?

2. How important is it to know that when all seems to be failing, God is still faithful?

3. Why does the outcome of Hannah's story of rejection bring us a sigh of relief when we first read about it?

4. What does it feel like to be second choice? What happened to Leah and Rachel's relationship?

5. Describe the beauty of falling in love with God to the point of total satisfaction.

6. Moses' unchecked responses to the actions of other people deterred him from fulfilling the

vision of his heart (or womb). In what instances have you lost out on a dream and promise God specifically had for you? What aspects of your sinful nature do you struggle to keep in check so this does not happen?

7. Abortion is a painful and uncompleted work. Describe how one might feel if they have aborted a spiritual baby.

PRAYER

Lord, I am so grateful that there is no failure in You. For this reason Lord, I place my every condition and my every situation in Your hands. Lord, take what others may have rejected and use it for Your glory. Show me how to cope with what seems like rejection and yet is Your plan for pulling me to go another way. God, give me insight to detect when the enemy is setting out to steal what You have already given to me. Help me to not reject Your plan for me. Teach me Thy ways. In Jesus' name, I pray. Amen.

Chapter Nine

Three Types of Wombs

THE WOMB OF NOAH'S ARK

And every living substance was destroyed which was upon the face of the ground, both man, and cattle, and the creeping things, and the fowl of the heaven; and they were destroyed from the earth: and Noah only remained alive, and they that were with him in the ark. And the waters prevailed upon the earth an hundred and fifty days.

—GENESIS 7: 23–24

HERE WE SEE that the womb is indeed a place of safety. In order to escape the corruption of the world, God (the original womb) prepared a man named Noah who would prepare an ark. It did not matter that Noah or the people of his day had never seen or heard of an ark before. For as long as something has already been established in the mind of God, it will (by God's help) make its way into the physical, temporal world. All God needs is an available man or woman who is truly willing to be used of God to carry forth His mission.

Noah was righteous and therefore his own spiritual womb was a ready vessel waiting to do the will of the Lord. Genesis 6:8 says, "But Noah found grace in the eyes of the LORD." Need we say more? Noah was different from those of his day. In a world that was captivated by the desires of the flesh, Noah had tuned his spirit to know the Spirit of the Lord. Therefore when God gave the instructions to build that which had never been heard of before to accommodate the rain, which had never been seen before, Noah did as he was told.

There is a tremendous benefit for following God rather than man. For Noah the reward was a gift to live through that which was designed to destroy all that was living. Noah was given specific details for building the ark. This ark became a womb of life and potential for everyone that entered. Outside of the womb, there would be nothing but death, while inside of the womb life was moving, growing, and preparing to enter into a world that had never been seen before.

In essence, the ark of the covenant became a temporary world, as all of the now living world resided within this well-maintained and well-protected place. Just as with a natural womb, Noah's ark was a haven as it kept its contents from the dangers of the outside world. Noah had been directed by God to pitch the ark within and without. This would protect the ark and all that was therein from the elements of the outside world. Just as the fetus is encased in the womb and protected from impurities and the dangers from without, Noah and his family and the animals were protected, as the waters of the outside caused all without the ark to perish, while they remained to repopulate a new world—a new womb.

This ark was an amazing womb as it promised and provided the perfect place for prosperity for Noah and his family. The womb of the ark was filled with life, joy, and triumph. This place would remain a haven until the time of deliverance. Just as with our natural womb, only God knew when this time would actually be. Until that time, God maintained the womb and life eventually came forth to a new and renewed place. This ark should remind us that God will always protect His womb. That is God will see to it that those who honor Him and live according to His precepts and examples will outlast any storm or any other hostile weather conditions. God will always protect his own, even if it means causing a man, such as Noah, to create what he has had no idea of before that moment. Again, God knows what is in the mind of man because God is the one who made man and gave man a mind with which to create thoughts and create things.

THE WOMB OF MOSES' ARK

And when she could not longer hide him, she took for him an ark of bulrushes, and daubed it with slime and with pitch, and put the child therein; and she laid it in the flags by the river's brink. And his sister stood afar off, to wit what would be done to him. And the daughter of Pharaoh came down to wash herself at the river; and her maidens walked along by the river's side; and when she saw the ark among the flags, she sent her maid to fetch it. And when she had opened it, she saw the child: and, behold, the babe wept. And she had compassion on him, and said, This is one of the Hebrews' children.

—EXODUS 2:3–6

89

What a beautiful image this is as Zipporah (the mother of Moses) entrusts her precious child to the womb of an ark. This place was another safe place. This mother needed a safe place because the enemy was after the fruit of the womb. Only by God's grace had she been able to keep this baby boy from sure death at the hands of the Egyptians. Outside of her own womb (her body) and then inside of her own home (another womb), the life of this baby was at risk. Yet God places in her mind (her womb of creativity) the thought to do something radical. Here, an ordinary mother becomes an extraordinary architect when she builds an ark. Zipporah builds a place that will hold and protect her baby from the outside world. Just as Noah did with the ark, this ark of Zipporah was pitched for protection.

It is so very important for the walls or boundaries of every womb to be protected. The moment that something enters into this sacred place, the life of what it holds is in great danger. So, no longer able to be protected by his mother's womb (home), the baby is set into the water. One more time we see that the water serves as an escape route for God's people. One more time the pathway for the ark is left up to God, as only God can control the winds and the waves. Then true to form, the ark containing Moses is guided to a place of immense safety when Pharaoh's daughter sees the ark, sends someone to fetch it, and opens it.

What Pharaoh's daughter was opening was no ordinary ark. It was the womb that gave birth at the cry of a baby boy. Just as any mother longs to hear the cry of her newly delivered baby, Pharaoh's daughter heard this cry and delivered the baby out of the womb of the ark. Just as a cry from a newborn baby touches the heart strings of those around, the cry of this baby caught the compassion of Pharaoh's daughter. This compassion moved Pharaoh's daughter to rescue the contents of the ark. Moreover, it caused her to love what moments earlier had been an enemy to her and her people.

It is important to note here that when God was about to do a new thing, He used an ark. The ark is a natural place of safety until the contents are delivered to its rightful place. The ark will always carry to safety that which has already been in the mind of God. It will always open up its contents to a brand new world. From there it is up to those within the ark to take advantage of what God has done and make godly decisions that will ultimately lead from one womb to another.

Just as Zipporah was led to build a womb for her bundle of potential, we too must labor to build a womb for the protection of all those things which God speaks to us about. We must never place in jeopardy a desire, a dream, or a vision that has truly come from God. Again, God is full of expectation. He is waiting to see unfold all that He has placed within our minds. He is expectant to see the fruit that will result when we avail ourselves to vessels (wombs) for the vision to come to us, through us, and toward others.

THE WOMB OF
THE ARK OF THE COVENANT

At that time the LORD separated the tribe of Levi, to bear the ark of the covenant of the LORD, to stand before the LORD to minister unto him, and to bless in his name, unto this day.

—DEUTERONOMY 10:8

That Moses commanded the Levites, which bare the ark of the covenant of the LORD, saying, Take this book of the law, and put it in the side of the ark of the covenant of the LORD your God, that it may be there for a witness against thee.

—DEUTERONOMY 31:25

And when they came to Nachon's threshingfloor, Uzzah put forth his hand to the ark of God, and took

> hold of it; for the oxen shook it. And the anger of the
> LORD was kindled against Uzzah; and God smote
> him there for his error; and there he died by the ark
> of God.
>
> —2 SAMUEL 6:6–7

> Which had the golden censer, and the ark of the cov-
> enant overlaid round about with gold, wherein was
> the golden pot that had manna, and Aaron's rod that
> budded, and the tables of the covenant.
>
> —HEBREWS 9:4

During the time of the Old Testament, God's presence dwelt in the ark of the convenent. This ark was in the holy of holies. This sacred place was also a womb. This womb could only be touched by men specifically chosen by God. Only certain men of the royal priesthood were designated to care for the environment or surrounding of this womb. On a yearly basis a high priest would enter into this intimate place to offer up sacrifices on behalf of the sins of the people. This priest could not enter into this womb in any old way. Instead, he had to sanctify himself. If he did not strictly adhere to the sanctification process before entering this womb that housed the presence of the holy God, he would be struck dead. For nothing unholy can stand in the presence of a holy God! "Sanctify yourselves therefore, and be ye holy: for I am the LORD your God" (Lev. 20:7).

As long as the tabernacle was stationary, the presence of the Lord was also stationary. This meant that the holy of holies was the fixed place or womb that held the presence of the Lord. This place of the womb was special because the people of God had a physical assurance that God was with them. They knew that when God's presence was with them, His blessing was with them to protect and guide them.

Even while they wandered in the wilderness, they carried the ark of the convenant with them because this is where

God dwelled. Later, whenever they stopped they built a tent that would serve as the new womb, or place of sacredness for God's people.

Later, when they moved from place to place, the actual ark itself symbolized the womb. This ark was so anointed that when it was mishandled by a man, he fell dead. (See 2 Samuel 6:7.) Only certain people could carry the ark. Only those of the priestly tribe could hold onto the bars that held it in place. From this, we can learn that a womb must be handled very carefully and in accordance with stipulations and limitations ordered by God.

The womb of the ark housed other treasures that needed to be protected as well. For instance, it contained Aaron's rod that budded. This rod was a testimony of divine favor for this tribe that He had chosen to handle His intimate business. The ark also contained the golden pot that held the manna. It was a reminder of how God provided for them in a dry and strange place. The ark of the covenant contained the tablets of the commandments that were reminders that God has a standard that must always be maintained by His people.

This awesome womb pictures God. It provides us a picture of the fact that God is Holy, He is our Provider, and He is a God of order. It helps us understand who God is, how He relates to mankind, and what He requires. The events surrounding this womb show us that no matter what is going on in any part of the world, He demands that His presence and person are respected and hallowed above all.

This ark was very, very important to the people of Israel. This ark housed the presence of the only true and living God. The One who would sustain them in the midst of all of their troubles. Even when the people were disobedient and full of complaints, God was still the same. This characteristic of God is assures us today that God will do for us just what He did for them. We can rest assured that just as God was faithful and unchanging in the days of Moses and David, He is also today.

Because God is unchanging, the Bible is the manual for knowing who God is and how God operates. We do not have to rely on our own faulty imaginations of who God might be. Rather, we can read the living Word of God.

STUDY/DISCUSSION QUESTIONS

1. In a world full of sin, how must Noah have trained his children so that they were able to choose to follow their father into a place that they could not have even imagined?

2. Based on the previous question, what do you think it will take for you to go to the "next level" or "dimension" in your spiritual walk in Christ Jesus?

3. How much do you trust God? Do you even trust the very winds to carry you to where God will take you? What enabled Moses's mother to put her baby in that tiny ark?

4. Why did the Israelites always keep this ark with them?

5. Based on your response to question above, in what ways can you apply this principle to your own life?

6. Where can your personal ark of the covenant be found?

PRAYER

Father, I thank You for giving us the ability to feel Your presence. God, I know that in Your presence there is fullness of joy and at Your right hand I can find pleasures forevermore. Lord, help me to seek Your presence rather than those presents I desire. Father, I want to love You above all else because You are all I need, and everything I need I will find in You. God, I thank You for helping me to understand that I can trust You in every way. Continue to lead me in the paths of righteousness for Your name's sake. In Jesus' name, I pray. Amen.

Chapter Ten

The Training of a Womb

Greatly desiring to see thee, being mindful of thy tears, that I may be filled with joy; When I call to remembrance the unfeigned faith that is in thee, which dwelt first in thy grandmother Lois, and thy mother Eunice; and I am persuaded that in thee also. Wherefore I put thee in remembrance that thou stir up the gift of God, which is in thee by the putting on of my hands. For God hath not given us the spirit of fear; but of power, and of love, and of a sound mind.

—2 TIMOTHY 1:4–7

HERE THE APOSTLE Paul is speaking to his spiritual son in the gospel, Timothy. Eivdently, Timothy is experiencing some difficulty in his Christian journey. As an excellent mentor should do, Paul does something of great importance. Paul sees as every mentor should see. For he looks beyond Timothy's present state and reminds Timothy of what resides within him. Paul reminds Timothy of the faith that has been passed down to him through the wombs of his grandmother Lois and his mother Eunice. In other words, Paul reminds Timothy of the maternal wombs that have been invested in his life.

It is important to note here that Paul knew about the faith

of Timothy's grandmother and mother. This tells me that these women were not hidden, but that their faith was well-known. So rich was the faith of Lois and Eunice that Paul uses these family members to jar Timothy to the reality of his life. For Timothy had within his own spiritual womb the genetic traits that had come down from one generation to the next.

Genetically speaking, Timothy was experiencing a recessive moment in his life. That is, rather than exhibiting all of qualities that were definitely within him, these genetic traits were dormant. These attributes or qualities were needed in the work of the gospel and as long as they remained hidden and quiet, the Kingdom would not benefit from the gifts that were in him.

The key move of the apostle Paul here is that he remembered. Paul remembered the foremothers of Timothy and he used this knowledge to cause Timothy to remember also. Paul makes Timothy aware that what is within him is a gift. This gift, like any other gift is not meant to remain with the holder. Instead, the gift is meant to be given away so that others may benefit from its use. So, Timothy has within him a gift, and perhaps he has selfishly allowed it to become dormant. Or perhaps Timothy had experienced some discouraging moments that led to the gift becoming dormant.

Whatever the case, even though the gift is presently still and quiet, Paul gives the needed direction that gets the mind of this young man back on track. Here, Paul is writing from prison to a young man who has imprisoned the spiritual gift within himself. The question is, "Who is really in prison?"

As Paul writes it is a means of setting this captured man free. Paul tells Timothy that God has not licensed fear, but has indeed given permission for power, love, and a sound mind to reign in his life.

Paul then speaks to the young man about his own imprisonments and sufferings. I am sure that once Timothy heard of Paul's experiences, his own conditions paled in comparison. Surely, this would lead to Timothy coming to his senses and realizing that he has much to do ahead for the Kingdom of God.

Furthermore, the relationship between the apostle Paul and Timothy was akin to the relationship with Timothy and his foremothers. Paul saw Timothy as a son in the gospel and so Paul took on the responsibility of helping his son over this bump in the road of ministry. This epistle (personal letter) of Paul to Timothy continues as it offers encouragement after encouragement. It is as if Paul refuses to let Timothy forget that he has too much invested within him to sit back and let it die.

So, Paul encourages Timothy to stir up the gift. It is so important for Timothy to stir up his own gift. For although Paul could encourage Timothy day after day and month after month, if Timothy was not made responsible for making a choice for his own good, he would always depend on the strength of Paul rather than on what was resident within him. Paul tells Timothy that this gift is so dominant, so powerful, and so overcoming that if stirred up it will be observable to all.

The enemy is out to silence that which is in the womb because the enemy does not want anyone to know of the power of God that lies within. Thank God for every true mentor who sees the gift within and also speaks it forth. A mentor who refuses to help their mentee live and succeed on their own is not really a mentor. A true mentor will encourage those under their care to attain to the highest level of spiritual existence so that their full potential will be revealed.

When Paul charged Timothy to fulfill his calling, Paul knew that he had fulfilled his own course. Paul knew that just because he was moving off the scene did not mean that he did not have the responsibility to water that which was in Timothy. For in the same way that Timothy's grandmother and mother were yet a part of him, Paul too would remain a part of Timothy. Therefore, even to this day, the relationship of Paul and his son Timothy is held up as an ideal example of mentorship.

STUDY/DISCUSSION QUESTIONS

1. Have you ever experienced a time of depression? Describe how you thought and how you felt and operated because of this depression.

2. How has God used people and their words to powerfully pull you out of a depressive experience?

3. Depression and discouragement are very powerful emotions. How might Timothy have ended up if he had not heeded Paul's advice?

4. In what ways would a male mentoring another male be different from a female mentoring another female?

5. What signs give evidence to the need for male mentoring in today's world?

6. In what ways did the generations before you influence the way you think and behave?

7. In what ways are you mentoring others? Why is this important?

PRAYER

Father, I thank You for the forefathers of this magnificent faith. Please continue to teach me by their example. Lord, I know that all things are written in Your word so that we may learn who You are and how You respond to us. Now teach me these things by Your Holy Spirit. Lord, teach me Your ways so that I may teach others how to know You themselves. God, I thank You for giving Your people lessons and training us to walk in Your ways. Continue to help us to let our lights shine before mankind, so that our lights will give You the glory which is due to Your name. In Jesus' name, I pray. Amen.

Chapter Eleven

The Womb of Tears

Tears are not just emissions that occur during emotionally powerful moments. Tears are usually the conclusion to a silently lived occurence, or a witness to a known, common situation. As tears flow they are often a substitute for what cannot be said at that very moment. It is always hoped that those who witness the tears will understand the full details of what is going on—without being told. Tears are in no way a simple emptying of one's feelings. On the contrary, tears are an unfolding epistle as they seek to tell a story that cannot be spoken by their owner at that moment. Tears allow the womb of emotions to be free to escape their safe environment. For once tears have been released, a certain amount of vulnerability exists. For that which was housed safely in the "womb" of the emotions of a man often have been seen by someone else. That is, what was safely tucked away in the womb of emotions has now been delivered out of a sacred place and now resides in a social, more public place.

Hezekiah's Tears

> Turn again, and tell Hezekiah the captain of my people, Thus saith the Lord, the God of David thy father, I have heard thy prayer, I have seen thy tears: behold, I will heal thee: on the third day thou shalt go up unto the house of the Lord.
> —2 Kings 20:5

> Go, and say to Hezekiah, Thus saith the Lord, the God of David thy father, I have heard thy prayer, I have seen thy tears: behold, I will add unto thy days fifteen years.
> —Isaiah 38:5

The story surrounding the tears of Hezekiah is an interesting one. It would seem from the verses found in 2 Kings that Hezekiah had been in the temple praying, most likely in the inner court. Hezekiah was "already sick unto death." Yet even in this state, Hezekiah knew what to do. Hezekiah found himself in the womb of the Lord. Hezekiah could safely bare his soul in the presence of the Lord God of Israel. Even though Hezekiah had heard the verdict of death from Isaiah the prophet, he beseeched God with the deepest of his emotions, from the womb of his tears. As Hezekiah prayed to God, the tears became the evidence of all that was within him. What Hezekiah could not speak, his tears spoke.

Even though God had pronounced a verdict upon Hezekiah, when God heard the prayer of Hezekiah and when God saw the tears of Hezekiah, He gave another verdict. God stopped the prophet Isaiah and commissioned him to turn back to Hezekiah with the updated information. So Isaiah went back to where Hezekiah was—in the presence of the Lord—and told him of the good news from the Lord. God had granted Hezekiah an additional fifteen years to his life.

With tears, Hezekiah had poured out his emotional womb, and with care, God gave to him out of His womb of compassion. Surely, Hezekiah said much, not verbally, but in tears and weeping. Words were not necessary because God understands the language of tears. Hezekiah spoke more with his tears than we read about. This message was enough to turn Hezekiah from facing the wall and turn God from having Hezekiah face death at that moment. The power and persuasiveness of Hezekiah's tears are a witness to what the womb of tears is.

Esther's Tears

> And Esther spake yet again before the king, and fell down at his feet, and besought him with tears to put away the mischief of Haman the Agagite, and his device that he had devised against the Jews.
>
> —Esther 8:3

This scripture reminds me that desperate times call for desperate measures. While some may see manipulation in this verse, I see desperation. Queen Esther is desperate as she finds herself before the king once again. What was she going to say this time? What different words could she speak to touch the heart of the king? Would the king permit her to speak again? Would the king hold out his golden sceptre to Esther? Would Esther win the favor of the king once again?

Much was hanging in the balance when Queen Esther approached the king. Already Haman had received his just desserts, having been hung on the very gallows that had been

105

set up for Mordecai. However, there was still a great horror that was scheduled to occur. For before Haman was hung, he had already acquired the right to have the Jewish people killed. This situation was nothing short of horrific. Therefore Esther risked her own life once more when she sought the favor of the king again.

Favor is powerful. One more time Esther, who already had favor from God, walked in and received favor from the king. This time though, Esther spoke with more than words. This time she fell down in tears and begged him. This time tears told the story of Esther's pleas. This time it was all or nothing for Esther. For if the King was not touched by her tears, then she and her people would be annihilated. Interestingly enough, Esther was crying even before the King held out the scepter to give her permission to speak. So powerful were the emissions from the eyes of Esther that the king immediately responded by holding out his golden scepter to her.

What had exited the womb of Esther's emotions that day was a message that was far greater than words could express. On this day the womb of tears was sincere enough and compelling enough to turn the heart of the king toward the heart of Esther and her people. Just as a newborn baby from out of any woman's womb catches the heart of even a stranger, the message out of the womb of Esther's tears effectively won the heart of King Ahasuerus.

JOB'S TEARS

> My friends scorn me: but mine eye poureth out tears unto God.
>
> —JOB 16:20

What is a man to do when his situation does not win the hearts or the compassion of friends? What is a man to do when the words of so-called friends are more painful than the open sores on his body? What does one do when there seems to be absolutely no one around to offer comfort?

This is the situation Job was in. What a change from being wealthy and wanted by everyone. Now he was poor and no one desired to be around him or lend him a helping hand. Though in his life Job had prayed for others and given to others, there was no one to pray for or give Job what he needed. Job had survived the loss of cattle, the loss of his children, and the loss of his health. Even so, Job had yet held onto the fact that it was God that had given him everything and so it was also all God's to take away—everything!

There was no hatred in Job's feelings toward God. In spite of all he went through, Job never cursed God nor foolishly accused Him of anything. Job's anger was aroused at his friends who spoke to him as though they were his enemies. These friends of Job really did not know Job at all. Even Job's wife fell into the trap of the enemy when she admonished him to curse God and die. Job's wife sought a temporary relief from pain in exchange for an eternal hell of suffering and condemnation. What a trade-off! No wonder Job told her that she was talking like a foolish woman.

Even after everything had been taken from Job, he still trusted God. After talking days on end with his so-called friends, Job had had enough. Job scorned his friends. Job now cries tears as a witness of his soul. Now is the time for words to be spoken to God in a language that would touch the heart of the only One that really matters. When his friends did not understand, Job was now heard by his God who understood him perfectly. The beauty of the womb of Job's tears is that Job found comfort because he knew that in spite of a loss of friendship, he yet had the fellowship of his God. After a while, with God hearing the language of his tears, Job could say with assurance, "For I know that my redeemer liveth, and that he shall stand at the latter day upon the earth" (Job 19:25). For this reason the story of Job's tragedy, tears, and subsequent triumph shows that the womb of tears will lead to a story with an ending that must be told.

JEREMIAH'S TEARS

> But if ye will not hear it, my soul shall weep in secret places for your pride; and mine eye shall weep sore, and run down with tears, because the LORD's flock is carried away captive.
>
> —JEREMIAH 13:17

Here is a man who was known for his tears. Jeremiah the weeping prophet had much to talk to God about, and what he could not pronounce with words, he proclaimed with tears. Ironically, as we read through the book of Jeremiah, we actually hear the heart and the tears of God. God is so disappointed and so angry because of the sins of His people that He makes it known that they will now experience His wrath. God, through the tears and testimony of Jeremiah's tears, forewarns the people of their impending times of bondage.

Jeremiah's womb of tears continuously issued out warnings and advice. However, these words of warning and wisdom were not heeded. When we read the Book of Jeremiah we cannot help but be drawn to his words of woe. To hear the words of Jeremiah and to see his tears was to know that within Jeremiah was a love for God and for his own people. Jeremiah not only wept for the sinful acts of the people of Israel, but he wept for what was to come—the acts of God.

All of the tears in the world could not stop the Israelites from disobeying God, and rather than appreciating that God's servant was in tears, they continued to live in rebellion of God. In chapter 13 Jeremiah reaches the place of resolution. Jeremiah seems to realize that as much as he has given out of his bowels of compassion and as much as he has painfully wept, there is nothing more he can do. Jeremiah was a faithful servant. God had spoken to Jeremiah and Jeremiah had spoken to the people, but the people would not listen to the voice of the prophet.

The Book of Jeremiah encourages us today to heed what God's prophets, preachers, and teachers have to say. The very existence of our own country today is at risk and we cannot afford to turn a deaf ear to the voice of the prophet or a blind eye to the womb of the tears of the prophet. Just as God spoke in days of old through the tears of His most trusted servants, He continues to speak to His church today.

A Sinner's Tears

And stood at his feet behind him weeping, and began to wash his feet with tears, and did wipe them with the hairs of her head, and kissed his feet, and anointed them with the ointment.

—Luke 7:38

As we look at the sinner woman with the alabaster box, we note that she spoke no words. Instead, her thoughts and her feelings were communicated with excellence. For out of every cell of her body, she had something to say. This sinner woman wanted the world then and the world today to know that she had been changed by Jesus. This change was so powerful and life-enhancing that all she could do was give her best. This woman who new the value of things, took something valuable of her own and gave it away. The ointment she gave had cost much, but the impact of the life and words of Jesus had given her much. What else could she do? So overwhelmed by Jesus, this woman sought Him out. She went to where Jesus was and chose this day to express to Him her gratitude for how He had changed her life. You see, those that were looking on still saw her as a sinner and a defiled woman, but Jesus knew the real deal. Jesus was up to date about her present state. While she may have still lived in the city, she was no longer a lady of the night.

I do believe that when the woman heard that Jesus was nearby, she entered a labor stage and began to desire to see Him. Then as the woman entered the home of the Pharisee, I believe that the waters of her womb broke and what gushed out of her eyes and her soul was great joy and great thankfulness for what Jesus had done for her—what no other could do. She did not need to speak, for her tears told the story. Before she kissed His feet, before she broke the alabaster box, and before she poured the ointment on Jesus' feet, she had already begun to do something. That is, she was already shedding tears and she was wiping His feet with her hair. This is a powerful message. For this woman who had used her feet for much mischief was now washing the feet of the man who had changed her life. This woman who had previously used her glory (her hair) to attract those of the opposite sex, was now changed and humbled herself to wipe Jesus' feet with her hair.

This woman had no need to speak. Everything she did, from kneeling behind Jesus to pouring the oil upon Him, spoke loud and clear. Jesus had done so much for this woman; the least she could do was give her best. I can only imagine the change that the ministry of Jesus had brought about in her everyday life. This type of change gave witness to the burden-removing power of the words of Jesus. This woman had been in a spiritual, emotional, and physical prison, but Jesus had set her free.

Rightfully so, Jesus on that day explained to those around that what she had done had given Him a true expression of thanksgiving for all that He had done in her life. This story of this woman shows us that we must be unhindered in giving Jesus thanks.

One of the powerful witnesses of the personal impact of any person on another is when one is brought to tears at the thoughts of how another has blessed them. To be so over-come with thankfulness to God for all He has done that the tears of our womb are automatically released is truly much much more powerful than any words we may speak.

JESUS' TEARS

Jesus wept.

—JOHN 11:35

Here we have the shortest verse in the Bible, yet it is probably the longest conversation of tears that have ever flowed out of the tear ducts of a man. What is it that is gushing forth out of the womb of tears within the very soul of Jesus? What can we understand Jesus to be saying, when He has not spoken verbally?

Here, Jesus is in the midst of a series of sad situations. There is Mary, who had been so sad because her brother had died. Perhaps Jesus is shedding tears because of her lack of understanding of what had taken place and who He was. "Then when Mary was come where Jesus was, and saw him, she fell down at his feet, saying unto him, Lord, if thou hadst been here, my brother had not died" (John 11:32). Mary had a limited understanding of who Jesus was. Mary understood that Jesus could have healed Lazarus even while he was near death, but she did not understand that Jesus was more than capable of "healing" Lazarus from death. She did not know that Jesus was able to deliver Lazarus in death. Now, once again Jesus would have to teach those that were closest to Him about who He is.

Jesus could have also been shedding tears because a crowd had gathered that also did not know who He was or the true power which He possessed. In addition to tears, there was also groaning and troubling in the spirit of Jesus. Jesus continued to groan as the crowds spoke of how He had done so

111

much, but was not there to stop Lazarus from dying. What a limited view they had of Jesus! No wonder He groaned at the sound of these words. The crowds thought Jesus was weeping because of His love and His loss of Lazarus. This could not have been the case, however, because Jesus knew that He was about to see Lazarus again.

The reaction of the surrounding crowds had to be a major disappointment to Jesus. For throughout His ministry, He had showed forth the fact that He indeed reigned over many "enemies" of sickness and disease—even that enemy called "death" when He had raised to life the daughter of Jairus, the ruler of the synagogue. (See Luke 8:41–56.) His tears expressed what He felt at that very moment.

There was yet another reason to weep. For Jesus was now nearing the end of His ministry on earth. In other words, Jesus had only so much more that He would do to show and teach the people about His power. It was important for the people to understand His power, because Jesus was about to leave the people this very same power and authority. What a disaster for persons to have the availability of the power of Christ, but a lack of understanding of how to employ it. Jesus' tears carried much meaning.

The tears out of the womb of emotions within Jesus also demonstrated for us the humanity of Christ. He was fully divine and yet also fully human.

Jesus also wept because of the condition of Jerusalem. Jerusalem was in a sorry state. They were on the verge of consenting (as a whole) to annihilate the Son of God. With the foreknowlege of this sensitive issue, and now seeing the people "turn" on Him with accusation regarding Lazarus, Jesus had cause to cry. The tears that Jesus shed that day were different from the tears He would shed in the garden of Gethsemane. In this case, the tears were about His concern for the people. Later, He would agonize over the grave decision He was to make.

This miracle of raising Lazarus from the dead was necessary as the final, powerful proof of His divinity and as the prelude for what Jesus Himself was about to do. Raising Lazarus from the dead would be a testament to the fact that He could and would raise Himself from the dead. Just as no one could deny a raised Lazarus, no one would be able to successfully deny a risen Christ.

When Jesus wept that day, He released and communicated much through the portals of His tear ducts. The crowd had it wrong on that day—Jesus' tears were more for them, than for Lazarus.

> When Jesus heard that, he said, This sickness is not unto death, but for the glory of God, that the Son of God might be glorified thereby.
>
> —JOHN 11:4

> Jesus saith unto her, Said I not unto thee, that, if thou wouldest believe, thou shouldest see the glory of God? Then they took away the stone from the place where the dead was laid. And Jesus lifted up his eyes, and said, Father, I thank thee that thou hast heard me. And I knew that thou hearest me always: but because of the people which stand by I said it, that they may believe that thou hast sent me. And when he thus had spoken, he cried with a loud voice, Lazarus, come forth. And he that was dead came forth, bound hand and foot with graveclothes: and his face was bound about with a napkin. Jesus saith unto them, Loose him, and let him go.
>
> —JOHN 11:40–44

Just as Jesus allowed Himself to express human emotion, our human emotions also need to be expressed at the right time, way, and place. Also, just as Jesus' tears relate to us what He was going through, our tears should be allowed to tell our story. Jesus' tears were a sign and an expression of His compassion, the same compassion that moves Jesus to act or work on our behalf. Our own womb of tears should also release an expression of our compassion and a vessel through which the compassion of the Lord flows. Like Jesus, our own compassion will be seen when we are moved to act on behalf of other people and serve them like God's Word teaches us to do.

STUDY/DISCUSSION QUESTIONS

1. Have you ever cried and gotten your way in a situation? How may tears cause a person to reverse their former decision?

2. Did Hezekiah's tears really cause God to reverse a decision?

3. Do you believe that your tears have ever moved the hand of God?

4. Did Esther play fairly when she cried before the king? Are tears sometimes necessary in a desperate moment?

5. Why did Job have to move beyond his tears?

6. Tears are powerful and seemingly contagious. Why is it important to not get caught up in the plight of others to the point where you are overwhelmed by their pain, plight, or depression?

7. The most beautiful tears are those of a repentant or remorseful sinner. Discuss what a sinner who is ready to repent is speaking through tears.

8. Tears have the power to "stop a party" (change the atmosphere). In what ways did the woman with the alabaster box change the very atmosphere of the house?

9. What does "Jesus wept" mean to you? In what ways were the humanity and the divinity of Jesus exhibited as He wept?

Prayer

Lord, I thank You for making it possible for me to communicate with You, even through my tears. Lord, except when I cry tears of joy, I ask that You would help me through these tears. I thank You that You will supply my every need according to Your riches in glory, by Your Son, Christ Jesus. Father, I give my tears to You this day and I move on to live in true prosperity. In Jesus' name, I pray. Amen.

Chapter Twelve

The Womb of the Tomb

THE GRAVE

Jesus said unto her, I am the resurrection, and the life: he that believeth in me, though he were dead, yet shall he live: And whosoever liveth and believeth in me shall never die. Believest thou this?

—JOHN 11:25–26

And when he thus had spoken, he cried with a loud voice, Lazarus, come forth. And he that was dead came forth, bound hand and foot with graveclothes: and his face was bound about with a napkin. Jesus saith unto them, Loose him, and let him go.

—JOHN 11:43–44

Then he took unto him the twelve, and said unto them, Behold, we go up to Jerusalem, and all things that are written by the prophets concerning the Son of man shall be accomplished. For he shall be delivered unto the Gentiles, and shall be mocked, and spitefully entreated, and spitted on: And they shall scourge him, and put him to death: and the third day he shall rise again.

—LUKE 18:31–33

For the Lord himself shall descend from heaven with a shout, with the voice of the archangel, and with the trump of God: and the dead in Christ shall rise first.

—1 THESSALONIANS 4:16

There is a common saying that tells us that the grave is the place of the most potential. The reason this is said is because so many, many, many persons die without having fulfilled the plans and purposes God had set up for them. Surely, they would all warn us to not let death catch us without having fulfilled our dreams and visions.

While there is truth to this perspective, there is also another twist on the potential of the grave. While it is true that the dust has returned to dust and the ashes have returned to their place of origin, it is also true that these same particles or elements which make up a human body will live again! Therefore, the grave has another kind of potential that is waiting to be seen, heard, and felt. Although through sin, the womb of the tomb (the grave) enlarges herself as if she were a pregnant woman progressing through each trimester of the gestational period. There will come a day when this womb will usher out every person that has ever lived. This resurrection will be as the breaking of the amniotic sac and the fluid that is released will be the flood of those that have died in Christ. Eventually, the grave will give up even the sinner, because all will stand to be judged at the throne of God.

THE TOMB OF LAZARUS

Jesus provides us with a preview of that great resurrection day to come, when He calls forth His friend, Lazarus. Lazarus had died, and was now dead for about four days. This essentially means that the natural process of decay or decomposition had begun to set in. That is, the bacteria which were yet living within his body had begun to feed on the remains of his body. This is the reason why those closest to Lazarus had lost hope even when Jesus, the Miracle Worker, had come into their midst. Martha readily agreed that her brother would rise again. She had faith to believe in the resurrection day of the future, that is. However, Martha and those near her did not understand that since Jesus was the Resurrection, and that any time He chose it was resurrection day. They failed to understand that Jesus embodied the very essence of resurrection so that at any time or at any moment a resurrection could occur. All Jesus had to do was speak the word, and His words of eternal life would bring life to this dead situation. It did not matter that decay and stink was the order for the day with Lazarus's body, for when Jesus calls things to order, all things must take their rightful place.

This day, as the witnesses stood all around comforting Mary and Martha, Jesus prayed. Jesus prayed because He needed the spectators to understand that when Jesus spoke to His Father, His Father listened and the will of the Father (which was also Jesus' will) was then done on earth. In other words there was an umbilical connection between Jesus and His Father, and whatever traveled from the Father flowed down to the Son, Jesus. On this day the Father released the power to bring about the contractions throughout the walls of the tomb, which would expel a dead man. This day, the spectators heard Jesus communicate to His Father and they also heard the witness of agreement between the Father and the Son when a living Lazarus emerged.

Things that we may see as dead, Jesus sees as having much potential. Things we see as impossible because of decay and deadness, Jesus already sees as a living and breathing witness to the power and authority of God. Even the tomb that has held a loved one has the potential to issue forth. Whether this happens depends on whether it is the will of the Father. It is never that it cannot be done, but it is whether the Father's will is for it to be done.

THE TOMB OF JESUS

Jesus was lowered in the womb of a tomb. His body was laid on a slab and it was neatly arrayed in swaddling grave clothes. Even as He was born in a lowly manger wrapped in swaddling cloths, now He lay in a borrowed tomb wrapped in common grave clothes. The picture is ever so clear. For Jesus was one more time about to bring the greatest gift possible to a world that was in much need. For in the humble, burrowed tomb of Joseph, Jesus was about to deliver to the world the resurrection and eternal life. As a baby, Jesus was the gift that was given to the world, and now as a dead man Jesus was about to be alive again, but this time as a living Christ. Just as Jesus was an example for us before the grave of how we should live, His life after the grave also shows us how to live. For after the experience of the womb of the tomb, we shall live again. Mankind shall live again to bear witness that Jesus is the initial Son who was raised to life again, and now we, the joint heirs of Christ, will also live once again. Just as no one would ever desire to give birth to a dead baby, the grave will not give birth to anything except live children of God. Just as we anticipate the birth of a new baby eagerly desiring to welcome them into the family, so the kingdom of heaven awaits for the glorious resurrection day when new citizens will be ushered into the kingdom of heaven. On this day the angels will welcome us, and together we will live a life of peace and joy together with Christ.

In summation, the tomb is a womb and this womb has an appointment date to be delivered of its most precious contents. Let us be sure that we have made our calling and election sure, for the day will come when this womb of the tomb will give birth on the day that is scheduled by the Father, for only He knows the day and the hour when the Son of Man shall return. In the meantime, we eagerly await as the tomb of the womb promises to bring forth eternal life.

STUDY/DISCUSSION QUESTIONS

1. Have you ever been in an apparently "dead" situation, and then seemingly out of nowhere, there is a resurrection?

2. Do we show a lack of faith in God when we think that a particular situation has reached a dead-end?

3. After burying Lazarus, what conversation might Mary and Martha have had when they returned home?

4. What do you think was more painful for Jesus: delaying in resurrecting Lazarus, or suffering the words He heard when He arrived after Lazarus's death?

5. In what way is the womb of the tomb a passage-way?

PRAYER

Dear Lord, I thank You for life. Lord, I realize that even death is a part of life, as we pass from this life to the next. Lord, I ask that You would help me to understand that You have created tombs as a passageway and not as a final destination. Lord, today I celebrate life as You have caused us to live and not die forever! In Jesus' name, I pray. Amen.

Chapter Thirteen

The Ultimate Womb— Jesus

And whatsoever ye shall ask in my name, that will I do, that the Father may be glorified in the Son. If ye shall ask any thing in my name, I will do it.

—JOHN 14:13–14

Jesus saith unto him, I am the way, the truth, and the life: no man cometh unto the Father, but by me.

—JOHN 14:6

Now unto him that is able to do exceeding abundantly above all that we ask or think, according to the power that worketh in us.

—EPHESIANS 3:20

JESUS IS THE focus of the Christian faith. This indicates that as we live out our lives, we each must keep our eyes on the ultimate example and leader, Jesus Christ. Jesus is the key to the success of this walk of life. In Jesus we will find everything we need to conquer the enemy of our soul and be more than conquerors.

It is vitally important to remember that the Father, the Son, and the Holy Spirit are three in one. This triune Godhead operates to help the Christian no matter what kind of situation they find themselves in. The men and women of God are never alone. God Himself communed with man in the early years of Genesis, the Son came to the earth and took over the communication with man in the early days of the New Testament, and today we have the Holy Spirit who has been sent to walk alongside us. This lets us know that the presence of God is always here and always willing to meet our every need. What a reassuring thought to know that while we live out our lives, we have the presence of God to guide us, teach us, and lead us into all truth. Thus, if we rely on the triune Godhead, we will never go wrong.

Everything we need is in the name of Jesus. Since Jesus came from the bosom of the Father and the Father has created all things, it stands to reason that all things are also in Jesus. The womb of the Father issued out the Son, Jesus Christ, and now in order for us to attain all that we need, we must go to the Father through the Son. If we need healing, it is within the very womb of Jesus—Jehovah Rapha. In the New Testament we read that Jesus demonstrated His power to heal any manner of sickness or disease. The healing was not dependant on whether Jesus could heal, it was dependant upon whether the people had the faith to believe that the work was done.

Every name that is attributed to God must also be attributed to the Son, because the Son came from the Father. This is a point of inheritance in that the Son has inherited all from the Father. In essence, the Father was glad to bestow His possessions upon the Son and the Son seeks to bestow all spiritual blessings upon us now that we have become joint heirs with Jesus Christ.

> The Spirit itself beareth witness with our spirit, that we are the children of God: And if children, then heirs; heirs of God, and joint-heirs with Christ; if so be that we suffer with him, that we may be also glorified together. For I reckon that the sufferings of this present time are not worthy to be compared with the glory which shall be revealed in us.
>
> —ROMANS 8:16–18

Jesus is also Jehovah Jireh in that He will provide all that we need. Since nothing is impossible with God, if God does not do what we desire, we must rest in the fact that it is not the will of God at this time. This brings us to the point that we are to pray according to the will of God and not according to our fleshly desires. If God is first in our lives, His will is our will. When our will is His will, we are content and at peace.

Still, other names of the Lord, like Jehovah Tsidkenu, Jehovah Shalom, El Shaddai, Sabaoth, and Jehovah Mekoddishken, describe the sovereignty and power of Jesus. As we look at the examples of healing throughout the Bible, we are reassured that Jesus has within His womb all that pertains to life, health, and happiness. Certainly then, His will should be our will.

Jesus' compassion and power is what we think of about the woman with the issue of blood. She only touched the fringes of His garment, but this act of faith yielded exactly what she needed when healing, power, and prosperity issued out of the womb of Jesus. Jesus knew that something had left His body.

Jesus' power to meet our needs in this way came from the Father, even as in the beginning of time God spoke everything into existence and everything therefore was. When Jesus went along to heal the daughter of Jairus, Jesus did not even speak healing. His actions said it all when He began to go with the father of the girl. Even when the news came back that she had died, this could not change the fact that Jesus had already completed her healing.

The centurion from Capernaum understood that such faith in the power of the spoken word of Jesus the Christ meant it was not necessary for Jesus to come to his home to bring healing because he knew Jesus only had to speak the word and the healing would be accomplished. Jesus was absolutely captivated by this faith and said that He had not seen so great a faith in all of Israel (Matthew 8:1–10). Like this man, it is important for us to be convinced that Jesus' power is limitless.

When we doubt Jesus' power, we put the brakes on the things the Father has already prepared for us since the foundation of the world. Although we cannot see what is in the womb of Jesus, we will see it come forth if we have faith that it is there and will be provided to us. Our faith is made right when the prayers and desires of our hearts are revealed and people around us rejoice over it.

Jesus Himself spoke that He is the light of the world (John 8:12). For us, this light can be an x-ray that shows us what Jesus has within His womb. With this x-ray vision we can combat distraction, discouragement, and doubt. When our focus is on the fact that we live because Jesus lives, we are the lights of the world that lead others to "the Light of the world," and to eternal life and eternal joy.

STUDY/DISCUSSION QUESTIONS

1. Life is challenging. We all have needs. Can we really find everything we need in Jesus? In what areas do you struggle to trust Jesus?

2. Have you ever felt "let down" by Jesus? What were the circumstances?

3. What evidence do you have that Jesus will meet you at the point of your every need?

4. In what ways can a person reject Jesus?

5. How can we depend on Jesus, even though we have never seen Him with our natural eyes?

Prayer

Father, thank You for sending us Your Son, Jesus Christ, and thank You for giving mankind a faith that transcends the natural sense of our vision. Thank You also for the fact that simply because we believe, we have been given access to the ultimate gift, Jesus. Lord, help me to value and treasure my relationship with Jesus and to honor You in all I do. In Jesus' name, I pray. Amen.

Chapter Fourteen

The Womb of More Than Enough

Arise, get thee to Zarephath, which belongeth to Zidon, and dwell there: behold, I have commanded a widow woman there to sustain thee...And she went and did according to the saying of Elijah: and she, and he, and her house, did eat many days.

—1 KINGS 17:9, 15

And Elisha said unto her, What shall I do for thee? tell me, what hast thou in the house? And she said, Thine handmaid hath not any thing in the house, save a pot of oil.

—2 KINGS 4:2

And they say unto him, We have here but five loaves, and two fishes. He said, Bring them hither to me. And he commanded the multitude to sit down on the grass, and took the five loaves, and the two fishes, and looking up to heaven, he blessed, and brake, and gave the loaves to his disciples, and the disciples to the multitude. And they did all eat, and were filled: and they took up of the fragments that remained twelve baskets full.

—MATTHEW 14:17–20

MANY TIMES IN our Christian walk we feel inadequate and unworthy. However, the message from God in His Word is that we do have all that we need in order to have a life of success and abundance. This can be understood as we take time to peer into the lives of the women and the boy portrayed in the scripture above. Each will show us that in spite of the downturns that life sometimes brings, there is still a way up. Indeed, God will not leave us nor forsake us in our time of need.

The prophet Elijah had found himself at a desperate place of need. He had been at the brook Cherith and it had dried up. Elijah was now hungry and thirsty now that the ravens were no longer bringing him food. At this point God told him to go to Zarephath where a widow would feed him. This verse is so very powerful because here God spoke a prophetic word to the prophet. Every time God speaks, it has already been done in His mind. Now it was about to be done for Elijah. Not for Elijah only, but through this act of obedience God was going to meet two needs at once. So, God spoke to Elijah about a work that had been done already.

The woman of Zarephath was in dire straits. She was about to cook the last meal for herself and her son. It is at this point that Elijah asked her for a portion of what she had. The woman surely wondered about this strange and irrational request from the man of God. However, at this point Elijah spoke a prophetic word to her, telling her to not fear because after she fed him, she and her her son would never want for food again.

What this woman had within her womb was the faith to believe that the God of Elijah would keep His word. It does not appear that this was her God, but nevertheless because she obeyed the request of God the Almighty, He honored her. Though she only had a handful of meal, this amount of food placed in the hands of the God who created the earth was more than enough. I would like to believe that following this miracle, the God of Elijah became her God, too.

Another woman who had more in her womb than she thought was the widow who had two sons. This woman did not realize what she had invested in her womb and that this womb was now about to burst forth with purpose. Her husband had been one of the students of Elijah at the school of prophets. Therefore her husband had committed time to the service of the Lord. This also meant that his wife and their sons were involved in ministry because they were under his care. When this woman came crying to Elijah, these were not tears of faith. These were tears of desperation and fear.

Elijah then spoke a word asking the woman to look at what she already possessed. That is, Elijah wanted this woman to look inside of her own womb because this was the place where God was going to bless her. Though she said that she only had a little bit of oil, God also showed us here that a little in the hands of the Provider would be more than enough.

One more time the key to the release of what is inside of that place of the womb is having the faith to obey the voice of God or His servant. The woman obediently gathered vessels, shut the door, and began to pour. She and her sons poured until there were no more vessels to pour into. God proved to this woman that she had enough within the womb of her home to bless her and her sons for the rest of their lives. This also shows us that when our family invests in God's work, He will reward us with fruit out of His womb.

In the New Testament is the lad with the two fish and five barley loaves. This was only a lunch meal for a child. However, God used this situation to show the multitudes that He is the God of all supply. When the disciples could find no food and no solution to the food problem, Jesus sent them on a mission. These disciples were sent into the womb of the crowd to find some food.

In the Gospel of St. Luke the disciples said, "we have no more but five loaves and two fishes...." Isn't it funny how we think that we have nothing, but God will take the womb of what we see as nothing and bring forth a supply that ends up being a supply of more than enough. In this account Jesus teaches us to hold up toward heaven what we have, pray to the Father, and then by faith feed the multitudes.

In each of these cases there seemed to not be enough resource for what was needed. However, these biblical examples show that the Father already has the supply. Everything we need will be met by the ultimate source, the Lord God. He may use resources to carry out His will (like the oil, the meal, and the fish and loaves), but He alone is the source of every good gift we receive. This encourages us to not be defeated by the appearance of our present circumstances, but to lift our need and our faith up to the God of every circumstance. By obedient faith we believe the impossible enough to do what He tells us to do so that He can provide for our need.

STUDY/DISCUSSION QUESTIONS

1. Have you ever felt depleted, yet God still used you? In what ways does God take what we consider nothing and put it to His own use?

2. Why must we be willing to give even when we feel we have nothing to give?

3. While keeping in mind the woman who baked a cake for the prophet, have you ever lost out on a miracle because you thought you were at your last point and had nothing left to give?

4. Is it always wise to give to others? In what instances would it not be wise to give to others?

Prayer

Lord, I thank You because You have given us all that we need to be prosperous in this life. Father, help Your people to be a blessing to others. Thank You for giving to us so that we may give to others. Thank You for supplying our needs and using us in the supply of the needs of others. Father, keep me attuned to Your voice that I may hear and obey Your instructions. Thank You today for all that I can be through You. In Jesus' name, I pray. Amen.

Chapter Fifteen

A Womb Revealed in Time
—Saul's Womb

And Ananias went his way, and entered into the house; and putting his hands on him said, Brother Saul, the Lord, even Jesus, that appeared unto thee in the way as thou camest, hath sent me, that thou mightest receive thy sight, and be filled with the Holy Ghost. And immediately there fell from his eyes as it had been scales: and he received sight forthwith, and arose, and was baptized.

—ACTS 9:17–18

Then Saul, (who also is called Paul,) filled with the Holy Ghost, set his eyes on him.

—ACTS 13:9

WHAT WAS IN Saul from the moment of his conception and even before he was conceived? How could a raging mass murderer become a roving declarer of the Gospel of Jesus Christ? How could a man set his mind to destroy Christianity and then inside of a week start a journey of increasing the numbers of people in that very religion? In short, it was already mapped out in the mind or womb of God.

Though Saul was a brilliant man, a student of Gamiliel, a Hebrew of the Hebrew, this did not stop him from having to stop and become who God had preordained him to be. God had made Saul the way he was. God knew how intellectual Saul was and how very passionate Saul was about the Jewish religion. Indeed this passion was absolutely necessary because God was going to use this same passion to propel the good news of the gospel from one end of the continent to the next.

As Saul, Paul had learned and gained knowledge that would be crucial to the expansion of the gospel. Therefore, Saul was about to give birth to a man who would be called Paul. Once Paul was born or released out of the womb of Saul, there was no turning back. Just as once a baby has been delivered in the natural world and can never reenter the place called the womb, once Paul was born out of Saul he was not going back to become Saul ever again.

Saul was absolutely born for the kingdom of God. He was just not mature yet, and it was not until he began that journey to Damascus that God stopped him with a beam of light and changed the direction of his life. Indeed, Saul (who had always appreciated education) knew that this experience was the ultimate lesson and he certainly was going to learn the lesson well. Consequently, Paul became who God had set him out to be, and that was the greatest apostle who ever lived. Paul, who wrote two-thirds of the New Testament, would live to proclaim that gospel he had once denied. Just as Paul was transformed, we too must be transformed. For Paul's mindset became one set to fulfill his ultimate purpose and destiny.

No longer was he impressed by himself or his education or his own zeal. Instead, Paul became impressed by a God who could stop him, teach him, train him, and then commission him. Saul was blinded so that Paul could be brought into the light and today we benefit from this experience. To perpetuate the purpose of Saul birthing Paul, we must continue the mission of taking the gospel message to the world.

STUDY/DISCUSSION QUESTIONS

1. With the life of Saul in mind, examine whether a person can ever be thought of as a "lost cause" for the salvation of their soul.

2. Take an introspective look at your life. You were not always where you are today. What now gives evidence that you became a different person after Jesus came into your heart?

3. Light is a powerful illuminator of truth. When we operate in truth (knowing all of the details), how can we then make good decisions?

4. Saul who became Paul was not a trusted man at the beginning of his ministry. Why must we prove ourselves to people before they will trust the message of the gospel which we speak?

5. Why do we not have the right to give up on people or make the judgment that they cannot change?

PRAYER

Father in heaven, thank You for how You make the impossible a reality. You can make anyone into a vessel fit for Your service. Lord, I submit myself to You and to Your perfect way. Lord, help me to change and then use me to change a city, a nation, and this world. Father, I want You to do Thy will here on earth, even as it is in heaven. Bless me today. In Jesus' name, I pray. Amen.

Chapter Sixteen

A Generous Womb

And Jonathan said to the young man that bare his armour, Come, and let us go over unto the garrison of these uncircumcised: it may be that the LORD will work for us: for there is no restraint to the LORD to save by many or by few.

—1 SAMUEL 14:6

And it came to pass, when he had made an end of speaking unto Saul, that the soul of Jonathan was knit with the soul of David, and Jonathan loved him as his own soul. And Saul took him that day, and would let him go no more home to his father's house. Then Jonathan and David made a covenant, because he loved him as his own soul. And Jonathan stripped himself of the robe that was upon him, and gave it to David, and his garments, even to his sword, and to his bow, and to his girdle.

—1 SAMUEL 18:1–4

To BE GENEROUS is to give out of one's own supply. To be generous is to also give more than one needs to give. Generosity implies that while there is no obligation to give, the character of one person causes them to give to another. We see a wonderful picture of this in the special friendship between a would-be-king (Jonathan) and a king-to-be (David).

Jonathan, who was king Saul's son, had much in his possession. As the heir apparent, Jonathan had only to ask for a thing and it would be given to him. In spite of this, Jonathan was no wimp. Instead he was a mighty man of valor who was able to almost single-handedly defeat an army that was determined to destroy his father's army. Jonathan seemed the natural choice for the throne. However, inside of Jonathan there was a well, or womb, of water issuing out gallons of a substance we call generosity. Because of a special kinship, a special bond, and a special understanding between he and David, Jonathan had an unusual understanding of who David really was.

Could it be that Jonathan never wanted to be king anyway? Probably not. Could it be that Jonathan saw his father's rage and irrational behavior and knew that neither he nor his father really belonged on the throne of Israel? Possibly. More than likely, however, Jonathan understood David so well that in his heart (by the Spirit) he knew that Israel deserved to be led by a man who was after the heart of God. Of all people, Jonathan knew how much David loved the Lord, and that from his very youth David had been trained to shepherd God's people. It certainly is logical that David and Jonathan spent countless hours recounting their ever so different childhoods. It would seem that the more these men spoke to each other, the more they were knitted together in an unusual way.

At any given point Jonathan was ready to risk the wrath of his natural father in order to save the life of a man who was like a natural brother to him. Jonathan took great care to spare the life of Israel's future king from Israel's current king. Apparently, Jonathan already viewed David as the king. Therefore, just as any servant must be willing to give his life in service to the king, Jonathan risked his life for his friend and his king.

The day David went into the palace to live with king Saul and Jonathan, Jonathan understood it. He had never seen his father make this move and He himself had never had a friendship like the one he would have with David. Out of his tremendous generosity, Jonathan gave David his palace home, his father's love, the robe that identified Jonathan's position of royalty, the sword that he had used to win great battles, the clothes that signified his position, the bow that had enabled him to defeat any enemy, and the girdle that had strengthened his waist to secure him. All this he gave from the womb of his generous heart.

Jonathan gave one more gift to David. Joanthan gave David the throne of Israel. No, not literally. However, the most powerful acceptance of any thing, person, or situation begins in the womb of the mind. All of Jonathan's gifts to David indicate the Jonathan was at peace with the fact that David belonged where Jonathan did not—on the throne as king of Israel. From that time forward, Jonathan lived to protect the throne in preparation for its rightful King, David the Sweet Psalmist.

John 15:13 says, "Greater love hath no man than this, that a man lay down his life for his friends." If there was ever an example of a man laying down his life for a friend, we have it here in Jonathan. Though Jonathan did not lay down his physcial life, he gave up a life of prosperity as future king of Israel. Such generosity is unheard of. Time after time, Jonathan protected David and rejected the poor attitude of his own father.

The generosity of Jonathan was never forgotten by David. Many years later David would also seek to be generous when he looked for someone left of the household of Jonathan so

141

he could bless the person. The seeds of generosity planted by Jonathan reaped a bountiful harvest when Jonathan's grandson Mephibosheth, who was lame on both feet, was lifted out of poverty and placed in prosperity. For Jonathan's sake, David blessed Mephibosheth and one more time a member of Saul's family lived in the palace and ate at the king's table continually.

To be a giver is to automatically be a receiver. According to biblical protocol, it is in giving that we receive. Surely, Jonathan's grandson received from David because Jonathan had given to David. The way David never forgot Jonathan's generosity exemplifies the fact that we should also return generosity that is shown to us. If we are the the first one to give, we will learn firsthand that it is a more blessed thing to give than to receive. Indeed, it will be given back to us, "good measure, pressed down, and shaken together, and running over" (Luke 6:38).

STUDY/DISCUSSION QUESTIONS

1. What led to Jonathan being able to give all he had to David?

2. Have you ever given to someone when you did not have to? How did this make you feel? How was your giving viewed by the recipient?

3. Reread the account of David and Jonathan (1 Samuel 18–20) and examine whether King Saul was perhaps more of a father to David than to his own son.

4. Did Jonathan give David too much?

5. Do you think that Jonathan had ever wanted to be king over Israel?

6. How is it that Jonathan lacked jealousy?

7. Who were the winners in this Bible account? Who were the losers?

PRAYER

Dear Lord, thank You for showing us how to give. Father, make me a living example of your giving. Help me to look beyond my own needs and focus on the needs of others. May I daily live to make a difference in the life of one less fortunate than me. Forgive me for the times when I have acted selfishly. In Jesus' name, I pray. Amen.

Chapter Seventeen

Miscarriages of the Womb

Have you ever missed something? Have you ever desired a particular thing and had it within your grasp, but now it is gone? Have you ever made plans, only to lose the ability to carry forth these plans? This is the image or feeling of a miscarriage.

Any woman who has conceived becomes a mind or a womb of expectation. At the first missed menstrual cycle, there springs forth the hope of a possible pregnancy. This woman even without confirmation from an early pregnancy test or doctor's visit has already envisioned a future of holding the precious fruit of her womb. Hopes. Dreams. This is what a pregnancy is about.

For a man, he too can experience a pregnancy of a different sort. Nevertheless it is just as meaningful. A man may dream of building a house for his family, dream of giving his wife and children all they could ever need or desire. Perhaps this man has dreamed of starting a business. He has seen the building in his mind. He has seen the sign on the building and he has already felt the taste of success. This man has gone as far as to secure financial support from a local bank—hopes, dreams.

But what happens when you are carrying something and you drop it, or it drops out of you? How do you handle it when something that was in your care is lost? There are many questions concerning natural miscarriages. Unfortunately, or maybe fortunately, there are not nearly as many answers. As human beings of logical thought patterns we want to understand why the undesired happened. We want to know what has caused the miscarriage so that future miscarriages can be avoided.

Why the need to avoid miscarriages? Well, they are painful. Miscarriages make a statement of failure to the one who was to carry and bring forth. Miscarriages speak loudly of unfulfilled dreams. Once something has been miscarried, it will never be gotten back. It is lost.

In the Bible there are numerous examples of what we shall call miscarriages. As we look at these examples we will see potential that was lost or miscarried. To view biblical miscarriages is to read about the lives of people and to ask questions like the following: How could they let that happen? Didn't they know that there was trouble? Why didn't they do something before it was too late? Over and over again we wonder how people miss it. How do people "drop the ball" and lose out on the very things that God has wanted them to have?

ELI'S MISCARRIAGE

Now the sons of Eli were sons of Belial; they knew not the LORD.

—1 SAMUEL 2:12

And there came a man of God unto Eli, and said unto him, Thus saith the LORD, Did I plainly appear unto the house of thy father, when they were in Egypt in Pharaoh's house? And did I choose him out of all the tribes of Israel to be my priest, to offer upon mine altar, to burn incense, to wear an ephod before me? and did I give unto the house of thy father all the offerings made by fire of the children of Israel? Wherefore kick ye at my sacrifice and at mine offering, which I have commanded in my habitation; and honourest thy sons above me, to make yourselves fat with the chiefest of all the offerings of Israel my people?

—1 SAMUEL 2:27–29

Here we have a classic case of not seeing the forest for the trees. Sometimes we are just too close to the situation, too close to the persons involved, and thus too close to see exactly what is happening right before our very eyes. The saddest of all situations is when there is a miscarriage in God's holy house.

As we look at the life of Eli, we see a man who was blessed to hold the highest office of his day. Eli stood as a representative between God and man. Eli made the connection, filled in the gap, and was the mediator between the people of Israel and their God. Eli represented all that was holy, and all that was sanctified. Eli was privileged to go to a place where no ordinary man could go. Eli could stand in the place called the Holiest of Holies and as an intercessory lamb. Eli could make intercession to God on behalf of the sins of the people. What a privileged place!

No doubt, Eli loved God. No doubt God loved Eli. Their relationship was obviously intact—at least at the beginning. However, there was another relationship that could not have been intact. This was the relationship between a father and his sons. Something was missing. Something was lost. For while Eli lived to enter into the presence of God, his sons lived a life which repelled the presence of God. Hophni and Phinehas had no problem desecrating the house of God through vile and profane acts.

What a vast difference between the stand of Eli and the expected stand of his sons. By all rights, the sons of Eli should have been the next to hold the sacred office of priest. By all rights, Eli could have operated in the office for some time to come. However, because of the miscarrying ways of the sons, both their and their father's privilege and right to the office of priest was spontaneously aborted.

The loss of position was not a desire of God. Yet, when we fail to walk in the ways of God we cause our own missions to be lost. All of the hopes and plans of God are contingent upon a human mechanism called choice. No, God does not choose for us to fail, or decide for our sons, or to miscarry. However, through the premeditated choices of mankind, miscarriages will happen.

The sad fact about miscarriages is that though they are never hoped for, they so often occur. Everyone wants to be successful, yet not everyone is willing to do what must be done in order that this success takes place. Failure is easy— just do nothing and failure will happen. Success is another story. Success takes a lot of work and one can never sit back and watch it happen on its own.

One must wonder in the account of Eli and his sons, whose fault was this miscarriage. Why did it happen? Didn't they see it coming? Well, as a priest, I believe that Eli assumed that his sons were watching him and that his sons would learn what it was to be a priest by watching him. Whether or not the sons ever really watched their father is open to question. However, it is clear based on the outcome of this account that they may have watched, but they did not learn. The sons never knew their father. Hophni and Phinehas did not understand the passion that their father had toward the things of God. This lack of understanding led to abuse of the house of God, abuse of their bodies, abuse of the bodies of others, and ultimately abuse of the potential that God had placed within their wombs.

What a privilege to have been born into the priestly tribe. Yet, because of a lack of communication between Eli and his sons, this natural ability of leadership was turned and mutated into a leadership of gruesome behavior and results.

It took another son named Samuel to have to go to the one he considered his father to bring to light the current condition of God's house. Samuel did not enjoy this moment. For how could one tell their teacher that they had failed God and that they had allowed their very own sons who had issued out of their bowels to cause them to fail? This revelation broke Eli's heart and eventually broke his neck. For the miscarriage of the lives of his sons was compounded by the horrific loss of that which he was supposed to protect—the ark of the covenant. In essence as his neck was broken, the head was somewhat separated from the body. This miscarriage is an image of the permanent separation and permanent loss of his sons and the ark of the covenant from himself.

Hophni and Phinehas had a womb of potential that was never met. Hopes, dreams, and desires of their own father would never be accomplished. The heritage of the priesthood would not continue to flow through the loins of these sons to their own sons. What should have been a natural gift was now never to be seen. This was a miscarriage indeed!

It was due to the miscarrying womb of Eli that God chose Himself another priest. God chose Samuel to carry on in Eli's stead. Samuel would pick up the position that had been

149

carelessly lost out of the hands of Eli's sons. Whereas the house of God should have been a safe environment for the nourishment of Eli's sons toward their ultimate purpose, it was rather a tainted place that poisoned the lives of these sons. No longer could God permit this atrocity to continue. It was time for an expulsion. Thus, a miscarriage happened as the boys were prematurely ushered out of the house of God and ushered out of the world. Surely, the word *miscarriage* can walk alongside the word *death*, for every miscarriage means that there is a death. For this would-be royal family, there was a miscarriage and death to the purpose which had been placed within them. Not only this, but the initial miscarriage in the death of the sons was directly responsible for the death of the presence of the ark of the covenant and subsequently the death of their father.

Parents must be very aware of their responsibilities. No, not merely their responsibility to God, but their intimate and immediate responsibility to God through the care of their family. This story beckons every Christian parent to take care to train and correct their children. For the results of the rearing of our own children will show forth results in the house of God. We must never train others before training those who live within the confines of our own walls. For where there is godly love, peace, and training in the home, there will automatically be the results of love, peace, and correct training in the house of God.

DAVID'S MISCARRIAGE

> And it came to pass on the seventh day, that the child died. And the servants of David feared to tell him that the child was dead: for they said, Behold, while the child was yet alive, we spake unto him, and he would not hearken unto our voice: how will he then vex himself, if we tell him that the child is dead?

> But when David saw that his servants whispered,
> David perceived that the child was dead: therefore
> David said unto his servants, Is the child dead? And
> they said, He is dead.
>
> Then David arose from the earth, and washed, and
> anointed himself, and changed his apparel, and came
> into the house of the LORD, and worshipped: then he
> came to his own house; and when he required, they
> set bread before him, and he did eat.
>
> —2 SAMUEL 12:18–20

To view the life of David is to be taught a lesson in every aspect of life. From his youth to his mature years as king, and even unto today, the lessons of David speak loud and clear. Most of David's life is simply a sample of joy. However, there were mistakes. Even so, the mistakes turn out to be beautiful lessons.

Such a lesson can be seen as we look at the account of David's deadly desire for Bathsheba. David was a mighty man of God. David was a soldier of excellence. God had given him the ability to fight against every type of enemy. Yet there was one enemy David had to learn to deal with on his own. The enemy was himself. Being a soldier by purpose, David was fit for the battlefield. However, one day he faced a force within himself like none he had ever battled before. David lingered in lust for lovely Bathsheba, he determined to have her, whatever the cost.

The price paid for the woman he desired was death. Uriah died at the hands of a plan hatched by King David. David's prestigious and admirable relationship with God died. And most sadly of all, there was a literal miscarriage of the child created from the immoral act of adultery between David and Bathsheba. The child died.

David, what do we do when our actions displease God? David, what can we do when our own behavior results in the loss of a precious life? Through the accounts of his life and his psalms David responds to both of these questions with the kingly air of excellence. He shows us and tells us that while there is hope for the prevention of a miscarriage, you fast and pray. One must be ever so remorseful for their own deeds that have brought about unthinkable results. David did so. He was in ashes and he cried unto God. David repented. David turned away from the thought pattern that had caused him to commit premeditated murder. He had learned his lesson well and hard.

Once the child died, David got up, washed himself, and ate. It was now time to move on. This is such a vital point after a loss. There is always a price to pay for disobedience. Sometimes the price seems unfair. However, one must always retrace the footsteps that led to the consequences of the sin. After that, one must move on and live on looking forward to the future. To live in a moment of miscarriage or untimely death is to abort or miscarry the future hopes for what still lies ahead. Just as David and Bathsheba went on to give birth to Solomon, we must know that after a miscarriage there is coming a day when we too will enjoy the gift we have desired. After this crucial mistake, God rewarded King David with a son of wisdom. We too can give birth to wisdom, following the experience of a miscarriage. God will reward remorse and repentance. For to repent is to turn away from carnal desire and to turn toward godly and eternal desires.

Michal's Miscarriage

And David said unto Michal, It was before the Lord, which chose me before thy father, and before all his house, to appoint me ruler over the people of the Lord, over Israel: therefore will I play before the Lord. And I will yet be more vile than thus, and will be base in mine own sight: and of the maidservants which thou hast spoken of, of them shall I be had in honour. Therefore Michal the daughter of Saul had no child unto the day of her death.

—2 SAMUEL 6:21-23

Here we have the first wife of David. This was the daughter of King Saul. In the account of the returning of the ark of the covenant, we see a great divide between the soul of David and his wife. Michal obviously did not understand the importance of the ark of the covenant to the Israelites, much less David's personal joy at the return of the symbol of God's presence.

David had a passion toward God. This is understandable when we consider that God had trained him in the pastures amongst the sheep. David had been groomed to be the leader of Israel even before he was anointed to be king. David understood how to take care of sheep, how to protect sheep, and how to love sheep. What others might have considered a deficit, David considered a labor of love. David took this training so very personally that he compared his duty as a shepherd to the Lord's duty as the Shepherd.

It then becomes clear that the return of God's presence to the people of Israel was of utmost importance. The return of the ark of the covenant was aligned with the return of favor from the Lord over Israel's many enemies. The presence of God meant that there would be no enemy who would be able to successfully stand against God's people.

As we see king David returning with the ark of the covenant, we see pure joy and exuberance. For one to have joy is one thing, but when it can be seen there is more significance. This is part of the problem that Michal had. As queen she could not figure out what would cause a king to abase himself through outward common acts such as dancing and singing. How could David have gone down to the level of common people?

In the eyes of Michal, David had dropped the standard of royalty. To Michal, David had lost his grasp of reality and had forgotten his position as king. Conversely, David understood that his kingship was given to him by God and he owed God everything he had. David treasured the presence of God above the place of the palace. David had a passion toward God. David would write songs and great poems about the God of his salvation. David knew that the one thing he never wanted to be without was the presence of the Spirit of God.

Yet, this David was rebuked and rebuffed by Michal. It was at this moment that she stepped over that ultimate boundary. Before this moment she had a life of great potential as she would be the one to bring forth royal seed. However, after this harsh criticism of David, Michal never had a child. It was because of her words that her womb never gave forth that which it was designed to do. Michal aborted her purpose as she spoke out of turn, out of anger, and out of line.

Michal refused to rejoice with her husband because even in marriage she refused to accept his faith. Michal never gave up the gods of her father and this resulted in her never really lining up with David in the way that would have mattered the most to him. This led to her demise, and consequently little is heard of her after this incident.

It is a serious thing to note that due to our refusal to rejoice with another, God might shut up the birthing of our womb of potential. Conversely, when we share in the joy of another, we open up the door for the same joy to exude from us.

It is clear that Michal damaged herself in a permanent way the day she abhorred the joy of King David. It is just as clear that King David went on to bring forth many sons and daughters, as he continued to bless God with all of his heart, soul, and might. We must never mock or despise the presence of God or the pleasure of another in the presence of God. For surely, "it is a fearful thing to fall into the hands of the living God" (Heb. 10:31). To David, Michal became the unclean or accursed thing. He never permitted himself to be intimately joined with her after her displeasure was shown. She never understood that the most intimate relationship David had was the one between he and God. By despising this relationship Michal excluded herself from being intimate with David, whose heart was after God.

STUDY/DISCUSSION QUESTIONS

1. Why might Eli have avoided properly correcting his sons?

2. Preachers' Kids (PKs) often talk about the more difficult life they have. In what ways are children of ministers more challenged than others?

3. Was Eli a hypocrite? Why or why not?

4. Do you think Hophni and Phinehas were ever trained by their father?

5. In what ways were Hophni and Phinehas neglected?

6. Would you ever want to be your child's teacher? Why or why not?

7. Why is it important to be on guard against our own fleshly desires?

8. Did a woman defeat David or did he defeat himself?

9. How does one sin or one lie lead to another and become a web that traps people?

10. What do you think was the reason God allowed the baby to die?

11. Have you ever experienced a devastating loss, but then in time found that because of the loss you are a better person?

12. Distractions occur when one is not focused. Is there a time when you became unfocused and ended up in a bad place spiritually?

13. Was king David unequally yoked with Michal? Why should the marriage not have occurred?

14. Should persons of different religions marry?

15. In the Old Testament, barrenness was considered a curse. Why did God choose to shut up Michal's womb forever?

16. In what ways should we follow David's example of repentance if we are to walk in God's will for our lives?

Prayer

Dear Lord, I thank You for every seed of purpose which You entrust to me. God, I pray that each moment of every day I will make choices that will cause that seed to germinate and bring forth much fruit. Lord God, help me to stay focused on You. Lord, help me to desire Your presence more than the presence of people. Father, let my light and the witness of my life shine before those around me. In Jesus' name, I pray. Amen.

Chapter Eighteen

The Devil Is After Your Womb

And Adam knew Eve his wife; and she conceived, and bare Cain, and said, I have gotten a man from the LORD.

—GENESIS 4:1

THE DEVIL UNDERSTANDS one thing very clearly and that is that he has been doomed to fail. For God told him in the Book of Beginnings (Genesis) that his head would be crushed by the seed of the woman. Therefore from the beginning of time, Satan (the devil) has sought to destroy the seed before it destroys him. Satan is so vehemently charged out to destroy God's seed that he has aimed to make a direct hit on the natural womb of the woman. Actually, Satan has gone even further! For Satan has deceived man to want to lust after their own kind (men with men, and women with women), for Satan knows that if he can distort the natural use of the body of the man and woman, there will be no way for that seed to come forth. In other words, Satan has made an all out attack on that which God has established (that mankind be fruitful and multiply).

If Satan fails to distort the mind of men into believing that they should not join with the opposite sex in holy matrimony to procreate as God had designed them to do, then he will go to the next step. This step is to destroy the seed, the image of God while it is nestled safely in the wall of the uterus. Indeed, what should be a wall of safety for this unfolding life becomes a world of warfare as the enemy is out to kill the seed. Satan has convinced multitudes that unless the fertilized egg looks like a human or can exist on its own outside of the womb, it is not a human being. The devil has deceived persons to think that the loss of a fertilized egg means nothing at all.

Satan realizes the potential of the womb. He knows that whatever has been designed to destroy his kingdom must come out of the womb. Since Satan is not omniscient, he does not know what womb will issue out a teacher of the gospel, a preacher of the gospel, or a mighty Christian. Therefore, he is out to destroy all! Whether rich or poor, black or white, or saved or unsaved, the devil wants that life that is within your womb. It does not matter to Satan that every aborted child is destined for heaven. What matters to Satan is that they do not see the light of day to live on earth to do damage to his evil kingdom.

Let's take a look inside a womb or two:

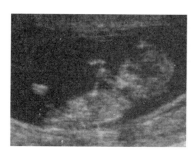 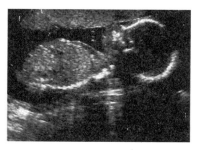

At this stage we cannot tell which baby is mine or which is someone else's. For at the earliest stages of existence all life looks the same. Yet even at this stage and before, God has already mapped out the entire life of each little person.

Time is the ingredient which begins to reveal the contents of the womb. For example, in the very early stages all fertilized embryos look the same, but soon the differences between the male and female embryo may be seen. Then, as the embryo becomes a fetus the physicians can examine an ultrasound scan to see if there are any abnormalities in the growth and development. In very much the same way, God looks at mankind and monitors their existence because He knows what should be seen. God is able to detect abnormalities in the lives of His creations, not by the light of scientific tools, but rather by the divine light which emanates from within Himself. I must stress again that at day one, hour one, second one of conception, the life journey of the union between male and female has already begun. As a matter of fact, the map has caused the fertilized egg to find its way to the wall of the womb and make its abode right there. The life of this union in its earliest stage has already been mapped out—completed, finished even while it rests securely in the womb. Therefore when one calls this completed life a thing, a mass of tissue, or an unviable cell, you are actually calling a completed life valueless. When someone aborts this "thing," the creation of God out of the mind of God is being aborted. This is because God has already invested His thoughts of creativity into this very life. To take authority over God's plan means that we just stepped into God's womb, or God's mind, and taken away life that He has permitted. In essence, we have just set ourselves up as God Almighty. Every doctor who performs an abortion has partnered with Satan in the plan to kill the seed of God—to kill God's image.

There is no excuse for an abortion. I am so sorry if you were raped. I am so sorry if the child is not healthy. I am disappointed that you think the timing is not right for this child to be born, but every fertilized egg in the womb of a female has already been in the womb of God. This is why those of us who have had miscarriages can be at peace and have joy, for we know that the DNA map of that child's life had in its coding that heaven was his/her destination. The child is safe in the arms of his/her Creator.

Just as every human being looks different so that each is readily and easily identified by their mother and father, God knows each of His creations because they are unique. The uniqueness of each person is a tribute to the wealth of potential within God, because we all came from Him. God expects each of us to be ourselves and not a clone or duplicate of anyone else. To ever "try" to be like someone else is to inform God that when He was designing you, He made a slight mistake. Also, to not fulfill our purpose is to inform God that His preordained will for us was an error. Of course, God does not make mistakes, for there is no shadow of turning with Him. God is perfect. Therefore that which He has perfected for each of us is perfect.

STUDY/DISCUSSION QUESTIONS

1. Can the spiritual womb ever become infertile? If so, what may cause this to happen?

2. The devil is surely after your womb. What will you do to protect your womb from destruction?

3. The first trimester of pregnancy is most crucial. In what ways will you protect your spiritual womb at this stage?

4. In what ways can you nourish the dream growing within your womb?

5. Multiple birthing is not uncommon in the natural world. What about in the spiritual realm? Can we carry twins or even triplets? What kinds of extreme care would need to be given in the case of multiple birthing?

PRAYER

Dear Lord, I come to You today to tell You that I love You so very much. Lord, to know that You trust Your creativity to natural minds is an awesome thing. Lord, I ask that You would show me and teach me how to care for all the things that You entrust to me. Lord, I exist to serve You. In Jesus' name, I pray. Amen.

Chapter Nineteen

The Womb of Jabez

And Jabez was more honourable than his brethren: and his mother called his name Jabez, saying, Because I bare him with sorrow. And Jabez called on the God of Israel, saying, Oh that thou wouldest bless me indeed, and enlarge my coast, and that thine hand might be with me, and that thou wouldest keep me from evil, that it may not grieve me! And God granted him that which he requested.
—1 CHRONICLES 4:9–10

A S I WAS preparing to facilitate a workshop, I was playing the song of the prayer of Jabez. This song was soothing to my spirit and it ministered to my soul. Then God began to give me insight into this wonderful passage of scripture. This personal revelation has caused me to understand ever so clearly why this prayer has become so popular in recent years. Indeed, this prayer is a key to understanding the importance of the womb in God's plan for man.

Jabez was a man with a spiritual womb. This passage actually begins by mentioning the womb of his mother and how she bore Jabez with sorrow. So it seems to me that even at birth, Jabez was in touch with feelings of sorrow. This obviously had an impact upon his life. Later in his life, Jabez called on the name of the Lord God of Israel. Jabez made a crucial request of the Lord. Jabez asked God to enlarge his territory and increase his coasts. The imagery I received here is powerful, as I saw Jabez as a man pregnant with a future—pregnant with purpose. Even as a pregnancy causes a woman to become enlarged, Jabez desired this enlarging. Even as a new baby would add to the family, Jabez asked God to increase or add to his coasts. This passage brings to mind the very growth and fruitfulness that is seen in pregnancies.

Jabez then asks God to keep him from evil and not to grieve him. Isn't this the prayer of every pregnant woman as she carries this precious and vulnerable growing life within her? The very last thing a woman wants to know is that evil has occurred to the unborn child or that there is a problem with the unborn child. The grief of a lost pregnancy is far greater than most can imagine.

The comfort of this passage of scripture is that God granted Jabez his request. This is like when that woman finally delivers out of her womb a healthy baby, for she knows at this very moment that God has blessed her indeed. At this very moment all is very right with the world.

Jabez spoke this prayer out of the womb of his emotions. He desired to live a life that was pleasing to God. His prayer signifies that we too should be asking God to bless us with pregnant expansion, enlarging our coasts in a way that God's hand of approval would always be placed upon our heads as we live this life. Like Jabez, even if we were born in sorrow, we may live in joy.

STUDY/DISCUSSION QUESTIONS

1. How was it possible for Jabez to move from this sorrow to wanting to add to the lives of others?

2. In what ways does keeping a pure heart toward others correspond with God's blessings being showered down upon us?

3. What is the difference between a saint being blessed and a sinner being blessed?

PRAYER

Lord in heaven, I thank You for the ability to increase according to Your divine plan. Father, I know that You give to me that I may give to others. So Lord, I thank You for the opportunity to give to someone else. Father, You can trust me to have in abundance that I may release Your giving power in abundance. I proclaim that all I have belongs to You. Continue to teach me by Your Spirit. In Jesus' name, I pray. Amen.

Chapter Twenty

A Salute to the Wombs
of My Life

But seek ye first the kingdom of God, and his righteousness; and all these things shall be added unto you.

— MATTHEW 6:33

A S I DARE to conclude this, my first book, I cannot do so without paying a written tribute to the many wombs that have caused my womb to give birth to past visions, this vision, and visions to come. The fact of the matter is that because God planned my end from beginning at the creation of the world, that I cannot even remember, nor do I fully know all of those wombs that have stirred up the gift within me. However, I shall make somewhat of an attempt to do so.

First and above all, I give thanks to God, my heavenly Father, Jesus, my elder Brother, and to the Holy Spirit, my constant Companion since my youth. I thank God that He entrusted my womb to carry purpose and see this purpose manifested. For surely my greatest challenge in life is to be responsible for the talents within my own womb so that I may hear from my Lord and Savior, "Well done..."

When I think of the fact that I was born to unsaved parents and yet salvation found my mother, my father, and me, I am in awe of how God works. God knew that it was a safe thing to place me in my mother's womb. Not only this, God also knew how to bring about a unique me; my life was mapped out before I nestled safely in the walls of the uterus of my mother. Though not saved, she cared for me, and both my parents nurtured me, so that the womb of my home fostered a natural desire for me to understand people and what was occurring around me. When my mother received salvation, the home became a newly enriched womb that ignited that "something" already within me.

To Grama, Juliet Simons, your early teachings of meekness have guided my life from my youth. Your quiet strength, patience, and ways of peacefulness, I adore. Thank you.

To Aunt Geraldine and Uncle Keith Lee, even before my mom was saved, you two carried me to church at Gospel Tabernacle, Evening Light, and Warwick Holiness. Thank you for the training and the introduction to feeling the Holy Spirit as He moves in people as they praise and worship God.

To Bishop, Rev. Dr. Goodwin C. Smith, I thank you for teaching me to teach others. From my mid-teens, I felt your passion in giving out the Word of God and how you wanted the people to "get it" like you "got it." Well, Sir, I got it, and I will never let it go. You have entrusted much into my care and I thank God for these gifts to me. Thank you.

To Mother Ruby Smith, thank you for praying about my natural womb's condition. It was a prayerful prelude to the manifestation of my first seed.

To Evangelist Yvonne Ramsay, thank you for recognizing a kindred spirit in the spiritual realm. As iron sharpeneth iron, we have encouraged each other in our separate pathways in proclaiming the Gospel of Jesus Christ.

To Pastor Dianne Tacklyn, after your very wise and sincere counsel, the Lord woke me up the very next morning and told me to write this book. I wrote and wrote until I finished it—inside of a three-week period. Lady, I thank you from my heart.

To Apostle Jimmie Denwiddie and Pastor Maybelle Denwiddie, thank you for always speaking into my life those things that the Lord invested into my being.

To Bishop Christopher T. Cox and Pastor Zulema, you guys are wonderful. Thank you for the encouragement.

To Pastor Leach and Apostle Leach, thank you for the very first publicly spoken prophetic words back in 1996, which have not yet ceased in unfolding.

To Rev. Dr. Barbara Austin-Lucas, thanks for your tremendous trust and encouragement. You are a fine example of what God will do with a willing and submitted vessel.

To Prophetess Marie Jackson, I thank you for intercessory prayer and a timing of encouragement that is truly divine.

To Evangelist Blanche Burchall, you are a gem to me. Your enthusiam is contagious. Thank you for getting more excited than myself about my accomplishments.

To my friends: Judy Marshall, Muriel Santucci, Marlene Somner, Cynthia Brangman, Gwen Smith, Shirley Hollis, Janita Burke, Terre Trott, Carol Burrows, Joanne Morris, Marynette Stamp, Maria Batson, Lisa Trott, Latanya Simmons, Rose Eve, and those I have forgotten to mention, I do so appreciate you.

To my sister Allison Russell, and my brother Raymond Russell Jr., I await for the birthing of your wombs into the kingdom of light. You have so much to give to the church. Thanks for your support.

Bishop Vernon G. Lambe Sr. and Bishop Neville Smith, thank you so very much for fatherly advice and care.

To Jenna Simmons, a spiritual daughter, I wait to see what you will become in God.

Mama Mary Maybury, Mama Ruby Woolridge, Mama Cynthia DeShields, Mama Phyllis Samuels, Mother Mary Hayward, Aunt Thelma Bailey, Aunt Thelma Burgess, "Dedicated", and The Berkeley Institute Family and Sunday School Class. Keep praying for me.

Mother Evangelist Joan Simmons, Mother Reverend Betty Furbert-Woolridge, Pastor Lynette Rayner, and Rev. Ruth Van-Lowe Smith, thank you for encouraging me in so many different ways.

Cousin Dr. Elaine Hodgson, thank you for your constant support. You encourage my soul.

Sister and First Lady Sheila Lee, thank you for a gift called "friendship." Pastor Lee, thank you for the ministry and encouragement, thus far.

To every friend, encourager, teacher, preacher, and pastor who has planted words of encouragement in my soul, thank you so very much. Thanks for entrusting your pulpits to the ministry God has placed within my womb.

Finally, I thank my husband, Kent "Peter" Eugene Seaman, a man whose womb is of great, quiet strength. Thank you for loving me enough to provide a place where I can birth and bring forth from both my natural womb and my spiritual womb. You have never stifled my visions, but have supported me as I have nurtured them and then given birth. You have covered me well. I love you and I thank you.

To those I have not personally mentioned, but you know how much you mean to me, thank you. I am reminded that no man (woman) is an island and that no one stands alone. Likewise, the body is made up of many members, and without the parts coming together to work in unity, I would surely fail. May God continue to grow us as we continue to unveil the plan He has for us. For just as the DNA of the individual is within the individual cell, the plan of God for each of us has already been established from the womb of God and now must become manifest through His creations.

DESTINY'S TREASURE

It seems I know where I am
Yet, I do not know where I will be
Nevertheless, I know those things I possess
And I know the one who possesses me.

For my past, present, and future
Have already been preordained
And every test, trial, and tribulation
Is really destiny's gain.

For I know the God above
Who is my Jehovah Jireh
No matter what state I am in
My God—He is my Provider.

Destiny—a future unknown by man
A thought, a dream, and even a mystery
Only time will perfectly unveil and release
Each gift and each treasure, God has for me.

So I hold on to my God
For He never fails
I await destiny's treasure to see
In advance I celebrate all of its unique details.
—AUTHOR: REV. DR. MARIA A. SEAMAN (1998)

To Contact the Author

To contact Dr. Seaman for speaking engagments or workshop facilitation, or to order her teaching and preaching CDs:

Rev. Dr. Maria A. Seaman
2 Mount View Road
Cox's Hill
Pembroke
Bermuda HM04
(441) 292-2435

Email: peaches@ibl.bm
Web site: www.mariaseaman.com